JERUSALEM
WITHOUT
GOD

JERUSALEM WITHOUT GOD

PORTRAIT OF A CRUEL CITY

PAOLA CARIDI

The American University in Cairo Press
Cairo New York

Feltrinelli Publishers, Milan 2013
Translated from the Italian by Yvonne Freccero.

Chapter 1, "Musrara, the Center of the World," was first published in *Jerusalem Quarterly* 62 (2015): 29–42. Reproduced by permission.

This edition published in 2017 by
The American University in Cairo Press
113 Sharia Kasr el Aini, Cairo, Egypt
420 Fifth Avenue, New York, NY 10018
www.aucpress.com

First published as *Gerusalemme senza Dio* in September 2013 by Giangiacomo Feltrinelli Editore, Milan, Italy

Published by arrangement with Giangiacomo Feltrinelli Editore

An earlier version of Chapter 1, "Musrara, the Center of the World," was first published in *Jerusalem Quarterly* 62 (2015): 29–42. Reproduced by permission.

Exclusive distribution outside Egypt and North America by I.B.Tauris & Co Ltd., 6 Salem Road, London, W4 2BU

Dar el Kutub No. 14203/16
ISBN 978 977 416 818 5

Dar el Kutub Cataloging-in-Publication Data

Caridi, Paola
    Jerusalem without God: Portrait of a Cruel City / Paola Caridi.—Cairo: The American University in Cairo Press, 2017.
            p.   cm.
            ISBN 978 977 416 818 5
            1. Jerusalem—Description and Travel
            915.694

1 2 3 4 5   21 20 19 18 17

Designed by Sally Boylan
Printed in the United States of America

To my son, Francesco Matteo Landi, who became a citizen of the world through his Jerusalem endeavor over the last decade.

CONTENTS

ACKNOWLEDGMENTS

This is a book full of ghosts. They are the victims, they are men and women who died in a daily, widespread, often hidden, sometimes eye-catching, never-ending conflict. Almost none of the victims had a resounding, familiar, famous name.

This a book full of the ghosts of friends who passed away. Before their deaths, they were our Virgils: they accompanied me, my husband—TV war reporter Filippo Landi—and my family in our dozen-years-long personal and professional experience in Jerusalem. Our thoughts and our gaze on the city would have been different had they not helped us: Father Michele Piccirillo, Bishop Pietro Sambi, Nicola Manduzio, Franco Scaglia, and, far from the Middle East, our beloved friend Toni Fontana.

This is a book where sacred and mundane stones are only the backdrop and sometimes the stage of the ongoing story. There, on stage, unfolds a very human history, played by the people, the invisible protagonists of my days in Jerusalem. I wish to thank them wholeheartedly, with a lot of nostalgia for having shared a whole chapter of my life with them. I will mention only some names, and I will leave some important men and women in the shade where they wish to remain hidden. For instance Michel, my Virgil through the neighborhood of Musrara, is the pseudonym of an old and gentle man, whose friendship I consider one of the most precious gifts Jerusalem gave to me.

Let me name the names, though. First of all, Raf Scelsi, Feltrinelli publishing house editor, who succeeded once again in convincing me to go beyond my reluctance and tackle an issue as complex as writing a book on Jerusalem. Eric Salerno, Sahira Dirbas, Michele Giorgio, Nabil Salameh. And Michele Lobaccaro, who surprisingly and smoothly helped me to understand that a secular person like myself could also speak about Jerusalem. Ambrogio Manenti, Tanja Popovic, Letizia Carracci, Carla Benelli, Osama Hamdan, Francesca Nardi, Francesco Battistini, Paola Pollo, Meron Rapoport, Susan Bino, *granpa* Avraham, Noha Brosh. Mahdi Abdul Hadi, Joharah Baker, Nasra Dahdal, Suleiman Rabadi, and all the College des Frères teachers, *hajj* Ali, Abu Majdi, *abuna* Ibrahim Faltas, the Muna family. Last but not least, our very special Jerusalemite family, the nuns' community of the Salesian Sisters in the heart of Musrara: Milena, Giuliana, Sabina, Caterina, Margherita, and the late Regina. My small and pugnacious Pickwick Club inspired, encouraged, and spurred me on, sharing the same passion for a very special city that wounds hearts and often mangles the faith of the faithful.

The English edition of my book would not have been possible without the passionate help of Lucia Sorbera and the professional vision of Nadia Naqib. I wish to thank Yvonne Freccero for the translation. And, last but not least, Kevin Dean for his patience and kindness.

My son Francesco Matteo Landi, to whom I dedicate this book, told me when he was thirteen, "You know better than me of Jerusalem's history, but I experienced the city by myself more than you did." He was right then. He is right today. I just hope that his very intense and in some ways defying Jerusalem experience will teach him to respect, always and everywhere, the dignity of each person he will meet.

INTRODUCTION: THE ANCIENT RHYTHM OF THE DAY

I thought and thought about what I would regret on the day I abandoned Jerusalem. Yes, Jerusalem: a sought-after city, mythicized, mourned, and yet so foreign to me that I would never, ever have thought it would become my home, my place of work, the setting for an entire decade of my life. A decade that proved the most demanding of my life, the longest I spent continuously in a single city—a closed city, walled and unreal like the Bastiani Fortress, which Dino Buzzati described so wistfully in his *The Tartar Steppe*. And I would take the role of Giovanni, Lieutenant Giovanni Drogo, who watches the years go by standing guard and waiting for something that has not yet happened in the long story of his tenure.

I thought about the city endlessly, even after shutting up my house opposite the powerful walls of Suleiman the Magnificent on a day in September, hot as September always is in Jerusalem. I felt nothing, no nostalgia; it was as though a door were closing behind someone after a long affair, yet I felt no regret. No nostalgia, even at that moment. It did not come until months later, on the steps of the bishopric of Mazara del Vallo, where I heard a familiar sound that had become intimate, in

1

its own way, in my life. It was cold, wintry cold, and the rain carried the distant smell and sound of the sea, opening itself to the west, roaring as in a perfect storm. And this sound, clear and alien, had the power to cut through like a saber and cure my bitterness toward a city that, over time, I had found to be cruel. "*Allahu akbar*, God is great," sang the muezzin, just beyond the white walls of the bishopric. The Muslim call to prayer that penetrated even a clearly Christian place, in western Sicily (so soaked in its own ancient Arab history), roused in me the sweet taste of nostalgia— the soothing sense of nostalgia.

Suddenly I discovered with a resonant flash that I did not regret the streets of Jerusalem, the sacred stones, the dazzling white of its historical architecture and the artificiality of its present architecture. But I missed the rhythms of the day. A clock's hours would seem to be the same every-where in the world, were it not that Jerusalem so very clearly and pre-cisely reveals its fate as a city in perpetual conflict. In so-called normal, conforming cities, time and space speak to each other, intersect with each other, and are almost never in obvious contradiction. It is not like this in a city that continues to be divided, despite what is said by at least one of the parties in the conflict, Israel, which claims the unity of a Jerusalem 'liberated' ever since 1967—that claims Jerusalem to be the country's one and indivisible capital. The reality is something else. Many architectural barriers that pilgrims have glimpsed on their swift journeys through the Holy Land signal the plight of the city and its inhabitants. More than its fragmented space, however, Jerusalem's sounds communicate the reality of Jerusalem. And if one withdraws from its difficult daily routine and stops to listen, it is possible to ascertain the plight of the city through its symphony of sounds.

In Jerusalem there are still times of the day that correspond to sounds and rhythms, that make for real moments to pause in the light but inces-sant beat of existence. Those sounds and rhythms are as ancient as the city: they are indeed a true and clear representation of it. Such as at the end of the day's cycle, the city is all set to lose the whiteness that is diffused in every corner, monotonous, almost like a hospital. When the sun is about to set, the sky is streaked with a delicate and luminous pink. It is no different from a Southern sunset, a Sicilian sunset, except that the event is announced by a song that rises in unison, and jolts us—us the inhabitants, the Jerusalemites—into paying attention to something beyond ourselves. Nothing escapes the distraction it asserts on our doings, our intimate rhythms. It is sunset, and everyone must know it, because in a few minutes everything will disappear into darkness.

The chant in Arabic is called the *adhan*, the Muslim call to prayer, repeated five times a day, not only to say that "God is great" but also to remember that our existence has a rhythm that cannot be forgotten. A rhythm in which there is a right time for everything, as we are reminded with disarming simplicity by the pages of Ecclesiastes in the Bible. The call to prayer is an ancient gesture that Catholics like I have forgotten. Yet it was an integral part of our day: the bell of Vespers has the same significance, reminding man that the work day is over and it is time to return home.

It is this measure of time that I miss: a day marked out not only and not so much by space, but by time, rhythm, and the sounds that interrupt life, reminding us, precisely, that life is time, deeds, a past that will not return, a present that is running away so quickly. It is as if these calls that mark the five prayers of Islam remind everyone, all the inhabitants of Jerusalem, and even me who is not a Muslim, how precious time and its intervals are. Fadwa El Guindi, an Egyptian anthropologist, expresses very clearly this unity—present in the Muslim world—between time and space. Rhythm unites them. "Rhythm is the construct that best describes this unity. . . . Muslims follow a rhythm in all spheres of their life—private and public, ordinary and sacred, work and recreation. Rhythm is not only a unifying idea, it integrates spheres of lived experience and brings thought processes and categorization of thought into it."[1]

Much more prosaically, the sound of the *adhan* is the natural rhythm that reminds the distracted. It reminds us of the dawn of a new day, that midday has arrived, that the sun has set, that before long we are going to sleep. Such marking of time is scandalous if you think about it, because this ancient way of dividing up the day is considered merely constrictive by postmodern man. Do we have to be restricted by archaic practices, precisely when postmodern thought considers the walls containing time to be completely broken down? We can eat when we want, wake up late, skip breakfast and invent brunch, be satisfied with a quick sandwich for lunch, and even eat late of an evening in order to see friends. We can skip the ancient rhythms and create our own individual intervals that are appropriate to us. Why should we be blackmailed by a preordained time, one, moreover, that is imposed by faith?

Nevertheless, even though my own time is overtly postmodern, still that call to prayer has been so precious to me that even now, when I am no longer in Jerusalem, it takes me back to real time, time that is more consistent with a nature we have violated over the years and centuries.

This rhythm is what I have inherited from the City of Three Faiths, attached to me under my skin.

The *Adhan* Wakes Jerusalem

It happens when darkness and torpor envelop the city, letting it rest from the rancor, the harshness, the humiliations, the madness that mark the days. As yet there is no suspicion that dawn is coming, that daylight is but two steps away, little more. A sweet sound breaks out every single day yet it is always a surprise. It comes out of the darkness, like incense. To listen out for it we must already be awake and our ears open, amazed at its sweetness as if every time were the first, and then wait for it to start.

The call to prayer rises subdued at first, then in a few minutes becomes organized like a chorus that includes all the minarets in the eastern part of Jerusalem, conducted—or so it seems to the profane listener—by the most persuasive and rigorous singing, the singing of the muezzin chosen to gather the faithful together by the Mosque of al-Aqsa, in the heart of the Old City. Al-Aqsa is the most important mosque in Jerusalem, the most sacred after Mecca and Medina. The "farthest mosque" as it was named in the Quran, to which Muhammad, the Prophet Muhammad, was carried on the back of a winged horse, the Buraq, in the company of the archangel Gabriel, and then carried back to Mecca after a visit to paradise. The muezzin sings from a place that in the beginning of Islam was the very destination of prayer, because in early times Muslims prayed in the direction of Jerusalem, and not Mecca as is now decreed.

It is a sweet melody that wakes us with grace, the *adhan* of the dawn. It is a call that gives the signal to more than the other muezzins. Jerusalem to the east of the Green Line becomes, like magic, the city's clock. The crown of little green lights—'made in China'-style—that illuminates every minaret becomes rekindled by the voices of the call to prayer, in a soundtrack that is always the same, as before every day that God—whichever God—sends to earth. Yet the amazement at this gentle and reassuring song is different every time, unique. It is sealed by the red fireball that will soon illuminate the summit of the Mount of Olives, just in front of the Noble Sanctuary where, together with al-Aqsa, the majestic golden mass of the Dome of the Rock rises up. There on the Mount of Olives, just beyond the campanile of the Church of the Ascension, the sun rises over Jerusalem with a rare and blinding glow: a light that hurts the eyes and gives the city back to space.

Listening to the chorus of the muezzins singing the *adhan* together at dawn is one of the few really mystical experiences in Jerusalem. As if waking the Old City, confined within its powerful walls, requires every morning only the ancient and moving call to prayer. While the city still sleeps and the sky is not yet light, the air, on the other hand, is full, happily filled with a collective and coordinated song.

Until the appearance of light, Jerusalem maintains an odd unity, each of its inhabitants confined to his or her ghetto: the districts, the houses, the inns, the convents, beneath a blanket of silence broken only by the sirens and loudspeakers of the military jeeps and police cars. Time is closed off between evening and dawn, a limbo during which Jerusalem can rest, and forget its obstacles.

The day, however, returns everything to a code of conflict. With the daylight, space wins over time, and again defines the roles within a city that is by no means peaceful. Space in Jerusalem is dominated by political presence, by the management of places by the Israeli authorities. Time and rhythm, on the other hand, are marked by two faiths—Christianity and Islam—that intersect each other at will in the air around the Old City. Christianity and Islam, in fact, share the Jerusalem of sounds. *Adhan* and bells. Calls to prayer and the ringing of church bells. Literary critic Jean Starobinski defines as a "bass line" this evocation not only of places but also of ancient *rhythms*: "Modernity does not obliterate them but pushes them into the background," in that they are "like gauges indicating the passage and continuation of time."[2] Judaism is silent, at least outside the synagogues. Author Ivo Andrić also says this, railing against a cruel and struggling city like Sarajevo, which also has experienced many identities. While the other faiths, by night, each in their way mark the cadences of time, "the Jews have no clock to sound their hour, so God alone knows what time it is for them."[3] Apart from the sounding of the ritual horn, in Jerusalem's rhythm Judaism emerges once a week with a siren that is not an alarm but is used to signal the beginning of Shabbat. A siren indicating a rite is a sign of how security is leaving a mark on the anthropology of faith—or at least of one faith—in Jerusalem. Urgency, emergency, and that danger that always threatens.

Those sounds of urgency are not just the distant sounds of the wars in which Jerusalem was involved between 1948 and 1967. They are the recent sounds of ambulances, police cars, and bomb squads. Sirens: first one, then two, then three, the fourth, the fifth. For a long time during the 1990s, and also during the Second Intifada, from the end of 2000 to 2004, the sounding of sirens in Jerusalem was the unequivocal sign of a suicide attempt, on a bus or in front of a bar. The rhythm of terror.

Listening Angels

The sounds of Jerusalem left an unconscious impression on me from the first days of my life there; sounds that had nothing to do with the rhythms of the day or of the religions present in the city. They were, if anything, normal anonymous sounds, attracting my immediate attention. The shouts of the market, muffled sentences, wailing, soldiers' commands, greetings, beggars begging. Like a crackling radio that melds several voices on the same wavelength. Like tapped telephone conversations. Like chatter on a bus, unexpected scraps of the lives of others. In other words, I had always thought of myself and the other foreign (and privileged) witnesses of Jerusalem as like the angels immortalized by Wim Wenders in that masterpiece of European cinema, *Wings of Desire*, a cult film for my generation. Wenders produced a much more complicated image of Berlin than a postcard snapshot. He removed the strong colors of the city that had in time become the myth of the post-1968 generation, choosing to film mostly in black and white. Berlin was black and white, which itself managed to describe the city and its inhabitants' marginalized and isolated condition, narrated in Wenders's film only by Damiel and Cassiel, the two angels who gather the silent and remote thoughts of individuals, in order to gather the soul of the city.

Thus for me Damiel and Cassiel are the singular, and in a way perfect, representation of the conditions in which I lived my individual and intimate relationship with Jerusalem for almost ten years. In this representation, with a healthy dose of simplification, I place the travelers, the journalists, the temporary residents, the owners of a passport that opens otherwise barred doors, formally neutral actors in a play in which all they had to do was appear. Witnesses, however, never just appear and are never neutral, precisely because they take on the responsibility of describing what they see, with that glance that is always unique and solitary. Witnesses such as Damiel and Cassiel are therefore also to be found in the city men have called holy, a little higher than others, very melancholy, within a body that is already in itself a free zone—a rare privilege. They circle above Damascus Gate that has survived all the wars and divisions, always retaining its function—the market, and therefore the center of Jerusalem life. They move to the east and to the west, crossing invisible yet very concrete borders that divide the city. They pass over the great periphery, built after 1967 so that the city could become Israeli as quickly as possible, the fulcrum as well as the most populated urban center of all of Israel. Yet the angels stop to rest, parking their wings and contemplating—from an old ledge or rooftop—the strange peoples of Jerusalem who brush against each other without touching, as they pass along the few streets in which the diverse community must inevitably meet each other, in this web of separate streets and invisible traffic signs that indicate to the residents where they may go and where, on the other hand, it is for 'others' to go, on that sidewalk, that pavement of the Old City, enter by that gate, shop in that store and not in the other one that is a little further away.

One can walk through Jerusalem, following the thread of its multi-millennial history, through the temples, the sacred stones, the boundaries of yesterday and today. One can admire the ancient traces and the new architectural buildings, take delight in the age-old and magnificent fascination of the Dome of the Rock, or shudder before Santiago Calatrava's daring tramway bridge and its steel cables that wind steeply up to the sky of Jerusalem in the direction of Tel Aviv. It is possible to turn a blind eye to the mystical power—real or presumed—that emerges from the white stone of Jerusalem. Or do something else. Close one's eyes and, like Damiel and Cassiel, turn on the tape recorder of one's mind, listen to the voices of the city, like the angels in a scene of Wenders's film between the shelves and the staircases of the Berlin State Library. One must arrive on tiptoe in Jerusalem, like Damiel and Cassiel, sometimes blind too, brushing the asphalt and the millennium-old stone, and listen to the men and women, those infinite worlds—not European but all Middle Eastern— who live, die, and sometimes find enjoyment in the city of their birth, or in the city they have chosen.

Just then, like the blind listening to sounds, one will discover the Jerusalem without God, the city of men and women, the earthly, not the heavenly, city. Just then, one will discover with certainty that Jerusalem is not a happy city, even when the dazzling June sun bounces off the white stone like a pinball, not even in autumn when the clear skies at dusk are suddenly lit up by a web of lamps and neon lights in the Old City, like an ancient nativity scene. The consuming moments of Jerusalem are lost in a sea of suffering, of latent conflicts, of injustice. The mundane wedding blessing of fireworks that punctuate the sky to the east every evening serves no purpose, nor do the concerts, to the west, in the municipal square, the bustle on Jaffa Road, the open-air mall of Mamilla, which follows like a postmodern out-of-tune hymn the ancient walls of Suleiman the Magnificent up to Jaffa Gate.

It is as if Jerusalem embodies the unaccomplished city. The city that does not exist. Yet the archetype to which it refers is the highest possible: the heavenly city. The paradise, as Cardinal Carlo Maria Martini describes it in one of the most beautiful passages of *Verso Gerusalemme*, his hymn to that most sought-after city, is not a garden but a world of human relations: "The goal of man's path is neither a garden nor the countryside, however attractive and fertile, but the city," because "the ideal city, the goal of man's journey, contains the best of the original paradise, the river of water, the tree of life: nevertheless it is a city, a place where men live in harmony, in a weave of complex and constructive relationships." It is a city where "there is a need for squares, for *agora*, where people can meet and understand each other and exchange intellectual and moral gifts of which no one is deprived."[4]

Here's the key issue. Jerusalem is no longer a city. Perhaps because it has no town squares. It is a place made up of walls that are physical as much as mental. It is there, in this incompleteness, that its cruelty can be found.

In the Uniforms of Identities

The fact is that many think they possess Jerusalem today. They clothe it in the sacred vestments of all the faiths, they often dress it up like a city that is only sacred. The Jerusalem of God, of a god that is exclusive for each of its faiths. To achieve this they wear the uniforms of exclusivity. They are uncontaminated uniforms, based on a single axiom: orthodoxy, almost always arbitrarily constructed. They are real existing uniforms people wear when walking out of their homes, because being recognizable is an integral part of their own balance and of what marks their place in the world. It is the uniforms that define the battalions, the patrols of these nameless armies that traverse the streets of Jerusalem. Men and women constricted by their clothes and by bald definitions: Jewish, orthodox, ultra-orthodox, secular, modern religious, new age. Veiled orthodox Jewish women, with cap or with wig. Soldiers with the *kippa*, who represent new arrivals in the Israeli army, whose bulk came instead from the secular segments of society. And then there are the Palestinians: secular and middle-class Muslims, peasants in traditional costume, boys in thrall to Salafism, devout rose-watered girls with matching shirts and pants. Possibly the Palestinian Christians are the most impermeable to uniforms, but not to the marks of recognition. They could be confused with other religious communities, in other words, were it not for the cross visible everywhere, tattooed on the wrist or arm, or on the garish necklaces of the adolescents.

Everyone has to be defined and pigeonholed. Uniforms allow anyone there to choose with whom to speak, to whom to open up, and from whom—on the contrary—to distance and defend oneself. No surprises there. Jerusalem is divided. Divided before and after the pre-1967 Green

Line. Even nominally subdivided within the Old City, where the invisible doors that lead into the quarters marked by religious membership are still there from the time of the British Mandate, because the European contribution to Jerusalem has been, paradoxically, the crystallization of division by religious membership. Muslim quarter, Christian quarter, Jewish quarter, even Armenian quarter—the Old City's divisions along religious community lines continue immediately also on leaving through the gates of the ancient walls of Suleiman the Magnificent. Jerusalem, divided by its urban communities, goes from the closed orthodox world of Mea Shearim to the white-collar sector of Rehavia and to the villas of the Palestinian notables in Sheikh Jarrah. It extends from the more or less permanent barriers with which the police control traffic even to the invisible streets that citizens traverse according to where they belong. Or presume to belong.

The formal concept, which is the most common in the City of Three Faiths, gives rise continuously to three diverse forms of dress, uniform, religious habit, hat, veil. The wardrobe is necessary to conceal each Jerusalemite with clothes that are 'recognizable' to those like oneself, and that are therefore acceptable: an impenetrable shell from osmosis, from doubt, from desertion, from sampling. Either here or there, or somewhere else, each person is assigned one's own role—a part in a play. Never stateless, never without faith, never multiple, never hybrid, never contaminated, never fascinated by the person in front. One must be pure, otherwise these divisions into airtight compartments cannot be justified when faced with intelligence and common sense.

In fact, if Jerusalem were not its 'myth,' those wrappings that cover its inhabitants would dissolve, revealing them naked to one another. And so, finally, Jerusalem would be a complete city. A place of contact and intermingling.

Speaking of the Real City

The Jerusalem of sounds, in other words, does not speak only one language. In fact, it establishes a diverse narrative of the City of Three Faiths, a complex narrative that is certainly not redemptive. It goes beyond the alibi of faith that many politicians have wanted to use as the excuse for a 'normal' earthly interpretation of the city. Conclusion: it is not a conciliatory narrative that begins here. It does not try to reassure anyone who still believes in the empty words that have been used especially in the last twenty years of diplomacy and generalized journalism. 'Peace' is the word contained in the very name of the city, and it is the first to have been abused, and to have lost the sense of itself, its *sema*. There is no peace among the few remaining olive trees in Jerusalem, nor will there be unless the contemporary history and daily news of the city are dissected, understood, rewritten, and reformulated away from the generally received truths, the slogans, the propaganda. The identities and memories of the Jerusalem of a hundred years ago have been bent to the interests of the parties, sacrificing the political and social history that is made up of many different pieces. Yet again, as often happens in contemporary events, complexity has been sacrificed on the altar of a simplified reading and of solutions based on those readings, that then fail, miserably overwhelmed by reality.

In this case, the example of Jerusalem is emblematic. The contemporary history of the city has been reproduced based on the narrative of each of the single parties. There is no common story; if anything there are parallel stories that, however, political and diplomatic players have often refused to read in order to apply possible solutions. At the basis of the thankless and distressing destiny of Jerusalem there is not just what has been defined as an infinite conflict. There is the myopia of anyone who has looked at the plans and maps of the city, the lines drawn and accepted by the international community with a disregard for people's destiny: their lives, their ties, their houses. The cynicism has not paid off, because without those men and women, the inhabitants of Jerusalem, nothing can be done. Peace cannot be attained. And peace, a lasting peace that puts an end to Jerusalem's war, cannot happen without justice. Justice must be attained for all, and not just for the one party that holds a monopoly on power.

Jerusalem has been defined by Israel as the 'unique and indivisible' capital, the place to which every Jew wishes to return 'next year' and reconcile a history plagued with persecution and flight. It has been, in fact, since 1967 a unified city under just one authority, which governs a people who were, however, in Jerusalem before 1967, before 1948, before the state of Israel, before the Zionist enterprise. Jerusalem belongs to many, not to one. It belongs to everyone. Jerusalem has diverse faces, apart from uniforms, apart from myths, apart from cardinal points, apart from the ancient walls and the concrete wall. Moreover, the layers that make up its thousands of years of history cannot be inserted or expunged from the narrative, wherever convenient. This city is not only Israeli, not only Palestinian, not only Jewish, Muslim, or Christian. Nor is it only Holy. It is also, if not primarily, a Jerusalem without God, on which religion has often been superimposed like a blanket to hide earthly and mundane terrain, in a constant contradiction between sacred and profane, which tests even the most solid faith. It is, and even often, a Jerusalem that seems to be forgotten by God, a city all the more cruel in its daily life for being considered an altar to sanctity. It is the icon of the faiths, but even more the distillation of a history the results of which, today, have carried away what was its greatest importance: the sense of the city. These houses, streets, stores, traffic lights, lanterns, sewers, words, trade, money that make up its body: that is what is unique.

1
MUSRARA, THE CENTER OF THE WORLD

As essential as water or the air we breathe, streets are the corridors of the soul and the dark trajectories of memory.

—Paul Virilio[5]

"The Cypresses Are Still There"

Michel looks at them, high up behind the wall that surrounds a four-story white building, and his eyes begin to wander, thirsty, trying to recognize the little that remains from his distant childhood.[6] They are ancient eyes, Michel's, folded under the weight of an eighty-year-old man. He is already tired from the walk uphill along a little street in the center of Jerusalem, just outside the ancient walls of the Old City. But his breathing is light, concealed by the slightest of smiles, gentle and innocent, because that anonymous little street in the old quarter of Musrara is Michel's 'memory lane.' That is what he calls it in his impeccable British English: "the street of his memory." The memory of his childhood and of the fixed images of 1948 that marked a before and an after, the hiatus in his life. And the hiatus of Jerusalem.

Michel looks around like a stranger. He looks like the passersby who use the little street to get to the offices of the Jerusalem City Hall, just over the hill where a large square opens up. Michel, however, has no urgent business at City Hall. His arrival point is his memory lane. He is there, after decades, only to remember. Memories rush from the mouth of that bent old man with the tidily combed white hair. His memory lane was called Baldwin Street when he was small, named in honor of the crusader king in 1918 by the British authorities, together with a committee that brought together representatives of the three religious communities to rename the streets. Baldwin was a gracious street at the end of the 1930s, full of villas with gardens. Look there, the house of the French consul, and then that of Judge Khayyat—large, very large, with a real park surrounded by a wall. Right in front of the Khayyat estate was the house in which Michel lived as a small boy for ten special years: from 1938, in the middle of the great Arab revolt against the British and Zionist immigration, until 1948, the year of the birth of Israel and the first Arab–Israeli war, the year of the Palestinian catastrophe, the Nakba.

The little house of Michel's childhood was a single story, like many in the small but important quarter of Musrara—a prestigious area that in successive censuses counted at least one hundred and thirty one- or two-story buildings, as well as churches, hostels, and convents. Musrara was a built-up area, triangular in shape, established around 1875 in a place whose name in Arabic perhaps means 'field of pebbles.' It is bordered to the south by the walls of the Old City, to the west by the commercial district of Jerusalem, to the north by the Orthodox Jewish neighborhood Mea Shearim, and to the northeast by the primarily Muslim district of Sheikh Jarrah. From an architectural point of view, Musrara mirrors the typical style of fin-de-siècle Jerusalem: local stones, sloping roofs on four sides, Arabic windows high and arched in the upper part, and metal bookend window shutters. Then there were the gardens: rose gardens separating houses from the street, and behind them fruit trees—pomegranates, almonds, mulberries, and medlars—and those tall and austere cypresses that have resisted wars, new inhabitants, and rampant speculative building.

Musrara was the first mixed district to develop outside the Old City walls, where the Jerusalemite middle class—Muslim, Christian, and Jewish

Ottoman citizens—lived and in time consolidated their day-to-day life. There they freed themselves from the constraints of the sixteenth-century walls built by Suleiman the Magnificent, which until 1873 were closed at night to protect the inhabitants from external danger. In Musrara, the class of well-to-do that had developed at the end of the Ottoman Empire in the decades preceding the First World War placed themselves at the mercy of the countryside and villages that ringed Jerusalem and furnished the city with vegetables, milk, olives, and manual labor. Michel's father, a representative of a new post-First World War middle class, brought the family to Musrara. An accountant employed by the British Mandate administration, he was accompanied by his family to his postings: the southern town of Beersheba, where Michel was born, then Bethlehem, and finally Jerusalem. In Musrara, Michel's family, Christian Palestinians, rented their house from a rich Muslim Palestinian, Ibrahim al-Ansari. "Renting a house instead of buying took place ever more often in the city during the 1930s," explains Salim Tamari, who writes on Jerusalem between the Ottoman Empire and the British Mandate. Renting a house was one of the signs of modernity that even Jerusalem, the archetype of a holy, celestial city, was experiencing.

Despite his age and the emotion concealed by his gentle manner, Michel bathes himself in distant memories. He walks through Musrara, along the narrow streets that still recall the old urban weave of the district before the tragic interruption of 1948. He passes the houses, remembering who lived there. He identifies every building with a surname, a trade, an outline of daily life, until he reaches today's Ha Ayin Het Street, which goes west from the Old City walls, past the Salesian Sisters' convent. The nuns there continue to operate a kindergarten frequented by Palestinian children in a district that is now only Jewish, and for the most part ultra-orthodox. Michel turns and looks up, indicating another two-story building. "This is the first house we lived in, here in Musrara. We rented it from the Giacaman family." The Giacamans, another well-known family in Jerusalem, had subdivided that little building into four apartments, with one shared water pump. Now there is a music school in the house, to which a crude extra level has been added. A little further along, where there is now a busy photography school that has a large area for exhibitions and lively cultural programs, the Bayartis used to live. "They were of Lebanese origin, hence the name," Michel explains in a subdued, muffled voice.

Michel relives the distant past as if it were yesterday: the steps, the people, and certainly the trees. "Yes, that was where the cypress was, in the garden of our neighbor's house. They came from the big family Dajani. The head of the family was called Tawfiq Wafa Dajani, and was a clothier. And there were his sons and daughters with whom we played every day." Michel smiles as he reels off the names of his playmates without any hesitation: Walid, Sa'eb, Aseeb, Nabil, Aida, and finally Naida. He was Christian, his neighbors Muslim, together in a street less than two hundred meters long, almost touching the Old City. In fact, only five minutes on foot separate the memory lane where Michel used to live and play from New Gate and the school he attended, the Collège des Frères. The most important private school in Jerusalem, it was founded in the mid-nineteenth century by the Lasallian Brothers, a French Christian order specializing in education whose institutions still exist in eighty-two countries, including in the Middle East. It was then, as now, the school for the Palestinian elite.

Michel's memory lane is today a street of overwhelming nostalgia, even though in his youth tension was not only in the air. Nearly two hundred meters of barbed wire divided the street in half. As the end of the Mandate approached, the British decided that to maintain a minimum of public order in the city, it was necessary to separate and divide the adversaries—with barbed wire along Baldwin Street, or with a metal gate at the top of the hill, where the Jerusalem city government is now, where those with permission were allowed to pass. These were the employees of various British institutions, like Michel's father, or those who worked beyond the checkpoint, in offices, hospitals, convents, or the plethora of buildings that (Christian) westerners had built since the middle of the nineteenth century.

The situation became unsustainable in 1947, however, as the end of the British Mandate neared and the United Nations recommended the partition of Palestine. The stories of the disruption to Musrara's life are familiar. The growing tension, the subdivision of the district into zones, the barbed wire, the fights. Clashes between Palestinians and Zionists intensified. There was shooting, even on Michel's memory lane, and the family—like many others—began to think of going away, of leaving the house for a day or two, perhaps even for some weeks, until the waters had calmed. And then, return. The discussions were daily: to leave or to remain, clinging to their possessions and risking their lives.

On April 9, 1948, news spread that there had been a massacre at Deir Yassin, one of the villages in the ring around Jerusalem, carried out by Zionist paramilitary groups, the Stern Gang and the Irgun. The number of dead is still part of the historical battle.[7] Whatever the real number of victims, the massacre unquestionably changed the perception of the war for Palestinian civilians. In Jerusalem, and Musrara in particular, not only did news of the massacre spread by word of mouth, but Palestinians were frightened by the sight of the survivors paraded through the streets by the Stern Gang and the Irgun. Benny Morris describes how after the massacre, the Irgun and the Stern Gang "transported the remaining villagers in trucks in a victory parade through west Jerusalem before dumping them in the Musrara quarter, outside the Old City walls."[8] Meron Benvenisti, the deputy mayor of Jerusalem in the 1970s, still remembers witnessing, at fourteen years old, the "disgusting spectacle."[9]

The Deir Yassin massacre was the decisive trigger for flight from Jerusalem's city center and the surrounding villages. Doubts gave way to fear. Michel remembers the morning of April 20 as if it were yesterday, the last photographic click of his memory. The night before they had slept less than two hundred meters from their house on Baldwin Street to avoid the mortars of the fighting between the Palestinians at Musrara and the Jews at Mea Shearim. They took shelter in the St. Louis French Hospital immediately in front of New Gate. They returned home in the morning to Baldwin Street to get their suitcases, took a taxi, and arrived in Beirut about midnight. Exile.

Michel and his brothers could not have known the significance of the journey. That was the last time they would run through the streets they had taken to school for the last ten years. As usual, they passed by the house of a British official on the corner between Baldwin Street and the one that was called St. Paul Street and later, after 1948, was renamed

Shivtei Israel Street, the street of the Tribes of Israel. Michel still remembers clearly the official's house and the small wall—though now in their place there is a tall building that can be seen kilometers away—behind which a puppy named Fifi would bark every time the children passed on their way to the Collège des Frères. On the morning of April 20, 1948, however, there was no school on account of the war. Nor was Fifi there barking, only a swallow on the little wall, wings spread, unable to fly. The children looked at it, wondering if it was dead, and then one of them hit it. The swallow flew away. "I remember it as if it were yesterday. It found its freedom, that we are still lacking." There was no rancor in Michel's words, only a sad awareness.

Since then Michel had not returned to Musrara to revisit his memory lane. And now, upon his return, he cannot shake free of the discomfort. It's as if one feels an interloper in the part of Jerusalem that became 'west' in 1948, unwelcome.

Pencil Marks on the Ground

On November 30, 1948, just a few months after Michel and his family, like almost all Musrara's inhabitants, fled and fighting exhausted the entire city, Moshe Dayan and Abdallah al-Tall traced in pencil the dismemberment of Jerusalem amid the ruins of a house in Musrara. It was a physical demarcation line for almost twenty years, impassable from 1948 to 1967: the time during which the city was divided in two, from north to south, between the newborn Israel and the Kingdom of Jordan. Neither Dayan nor al-Tall could have known that the long wound they traced in the pavement of a dilapidated house would pass into Jerusalem's history as the most quoted and untouchable line (at least formally) of the city. And what had been one of the richest middle-class districts of the city would never be the same.

The line drawn by Dayan and al-Tall separated the Israeli army and the Jordanian Arab Legion, which for months had fought each other through the streets of the city. It was a front line. Through many twists and turns Dayan and al-Tall decided the fate of Jerusalem. Jerusalem's composite society was not the only victim. From the geopolitical point of view, too, the Israeli Dayan and the Jordanian al-Tall embodied the protagonists of Jerusalem's division, making a clean sweep of other political participants. The Israeli–Jordanian agreement excluded the other Arab countries, the remnants of the British Empire, and, partially, the United Nations. According to historian Avi Shlaim, the city that was "the scene of some of the fiercest and bloodiest fighting of the entire war, was quietly partitioned between the two sides along the cease-fire line in order to pre-empt the United Nations' move to turn it into an international city."[10] Say goodbye to the 1947 United Nations partition plan and with it the *corpus separatum*, and the idea that Jerusalem could not merely be divided between two national communities, that above all Jerusalem could be a city for everyone, and for the whole world.

Dayan, in his memoirs, emphasized the annoyance—his own and, he claimed, al-Tall's—felt during the international mediation on the ceasefire. During one of the meetings, irked by the contribution of the United Nations representative, the American colonel Roger Carlson, Dayan asked his Jordanian colleague to abandon the gathering and go speak in another room. According to Dayan, al-Tall "said yes, and to the surprise of all those present, four officials in every delegation, and almost half a dozen UN observers, we got up and left. In our one-on-one consultation we very rapidly overcame our differences, returned to the gathering, and announced our agreement that became the protocol."[11]

After that, Musrara would never be the same. Reduced and split by the Green Line, it was fragmented into three pieces: the most important part from the residential perspective would remain in the west, the central zone would remain for almost twenty years a no-man's-land, and the more commercial area to the east of the Green Line would remain with its back to Damascus Gate. The little houses of Musrara are today a memento of pre-1948 Jerusalem, and a living portrayal of how the city has changed over the course of decades.

With Musrara's division there died a certain idea of Jerusalem, with its districts *extra moenia* that converge toward the Old City. The fulcrum of the community, the market, the holy places, the exchange, they were all still there. The city-fortress was still the center around which life revolved. The ceasefire line, however, removed the heart of Jerusalem from what was defined as the 'new city,' the west. The armistice plan followed, for hundreds of meters, the Old City walls, which became ramparts for the Jordanian soldiers overseeing the truce. The *center* thus became a *boundary*.

A little to the north, still along the line traced by Dayan and al-Tall, on the outskirts of Musrara, is the Mandelbaum House. For nineteen years it was the only crossing point linking the city's two sides. The only crossing point, at least for the fortunate few who could cross the demarcation line between east and west. The house of Simcha Mandelbaum also belonged to a family—Jewish this time—who had chosen to leave the crowded and unlivable Old City and buy a piece of land further north, outside Damascus Gate. The Mandelbaums built a small three-story house, clearly visible even today from what the inhabitants of Jerusalem call Road No. 1, the four-lane axis that cuts the city from north to south. Built after 1967, it is the busiest road in Jerusalem and more or less follows the Green Line in its most important stretch.

It is a street that marks the definitive alteration of Jerusalem's networks of movement. For centuries before 1948, the Old City was the fulcrum from which streets left in all directions to important urban centers. Jaffa Street, Hebron Street, Nablus Street. After the division of Jerusalem, these streets lost their relevance; the Old City was no longer the heart but an atrophying appendage, set aside near the Green Line. Especially after the 1967 war and the constant stretching of the city boundaries, the Old City became a small tessera in a new, increasingly extensive mosaic of Jerusalem.

The Mandelbaum House, now renovated as a yeshiva, a Jewish school at the border of the Mea Shearim neighborhood, remains a sort of outpost along Road No. 1, in front of the large Israeli hotels that have been built on no-man's-land and that accommodate hosts of Christian pilgrims, Israeli settlers, and Jewish–American tourists. Over the years, it was frequently an outpost in the clash of communities in Palestine: in 1929, during the Great Arab Revolt of 1936–39, and in the war of 1948. During the first Arab–Israeli war, the house was often used by armed men of the Haganah, prompting the family to leave the building. They were just in time: on April 14, 1948, Jordanian legionnaires attacked the building, using explosives, and killed thirty-five Haganah fighters.[12] April was indeed the cruelest month in 1948, in the wasteland that was the heart of Jerusalem. The day before the attack on the Mandelbaum House, a convoy of doctors and nurses escorted by Haganah forces were ambushed on their way to the Hadassah Hospital on Mt. Scopus. The attack was revenge for the Deir Yassin massacre. There were seventy-nine dead, their names inscribed on a memorial stone at the top of the street, almost forgotten today where it stands not ten meters from one of the radical Israeli settlements in East Jerusalem. Like Palermo in Roberto Alajmo's description, Jerusalem is a city of tombstones and plaques that are more conceptual than physical. It is a route marked by struggles and stone slabs, a pilgrimage among the dead.[13]

Outside the Walls

Once upon a time, before the 1948 tragedy, Jerusalem tried to be a modern city. The Ottoman Empire found itself reforming and revising the administrative, political, and socioeconomic management of the Levant. It was a turbulent period that straddled decades in the mid-nineteenth century, starting from the Tanzimat movement for internal reform, passing through the conquest of Jerusalem by the founder of modern Egypt, Muhammad 'Ali Pasha, up to the Ottoman reconquest. The administrative restructuring of the empire that followed brought with it the municipality of Jerusalem. In the second half of the nineteenth century, Jerusalem—holy and iconic, but at the same time economically marginal—assumed a much more clearly defined dimension. Its *sanjak*, the province of the empire that extended from Jaffa to Beersheba, passing through Hebron and Gaza, became more relevant, and the city itself assumed an institutional and socioeconomic aspect different from that in the past.

The last decades of the Sublime Porte marked the emergence of a local political and economic society that negotiated its spheres of action with the central power of Istanbul. It was not only the Palestinian notables, the great families, who managed their relationship with the Turkish administration. The real change was in the birth of the municipality, and therefore in the formation of the council and in the new figure of the mayor. Far from being the long arm of Ottoman power, the town council became the instrument for changing the city. It was the communal administration that intruded on the daily life of the city, first, determining and creating infrastructure and, second, becoming the referents of a community of Ottoman citizens that included the various religious denominations.[14] After the Crimean War and the 1856 Treaty of Paris ended the Russian monopoly over Christians in the Ottoman Empire, France, Great Britain, and Prussia entered into the political management of Christian interests in Jerusalem. The European powers gradually imposed their presence in Jerusalem, waiting for the day that the Holy City would no longer be under Istanbul. Each anxious to demonstrate its own national genius, France, Great Britain, Russia, Prussia, and to a much lesser degree Italy set their architects and masons to work in Jerusalem. The increased European presence in the city was aesthetic as well as political.

The difference did not go unnoticed. In 1897, Frenchman Victor Guérin published the first volume of his description of the Holy Land, of the scenery, the cities, and the religions. His was not just a description of a pilgrimage but a study of the social, economic, and political development of the city at the end of the nineteenth century:

> What is immediately clear today to the eyes of a pilgrim just arriving in Jerusalem from Jaffa, are the huge constructions of the Russians, a kind of citadel that is also political and religious, built at the gates of the city, in the very place where the city has always been and where it will always be attacked. Its erection appears as a threat of the schism and of the Muscovite Empire that aspired more than ever to take hold of the Holy Places.[15]

When it was constructed a century and a half ago, the so-called Russian compound was meant to serve various purposes. From a strictly religious point of view, it served to accommodate Russian Orthodox pilgrims. From a political angle, it showed, by the architectural strength of its buildings, the power of Moscow in the Holy Land and in confrontation with the declining Ottoman Empire. Last but not least, it affirmed that Russia also had a say in the future of Jerusalem, as Guérin noted. From a much more mundane perspective, the imposing Russian compound—at one time comprising a church, hospital, hostel, and convent—has been adapted to various uses by Israeli institutions. It hosts the City Hall's offices, as well as the police station infamous to Palestinians. For them, it is to the notorious Muskubiyah that prisoners are taken for interrogation, at times for days in isolation.

The "huge constructions" of the compound are clearly visible on maps Guérin drew in 1881. The imposing buildings are not far from the Old City walls. Also outside the walls, Guérin noted "schools and hospitals recently founded by Prussia and England, visible testimonies of the efforts made by heresy to dispute Catholicism's sole possession of the sacred land. . . . There are, moreover, private houses, consulates, gardens, and even cafés."[16] They are marked "Maisons Nouvelles et Jardins" on the map between the Russian compound and the Old City. Those "Maisons Nouvelles et Jardins" were the first nucleus of Musrara. Private houses and consulates, houses of important or rich families that wanted to leave the narrow spaces and small houses of the Old City, the overcrowding and the irresolvable infrastructural problems that resulted.

This community of petit bourgeois and middle-class Palestinians, mostly Christians but also Muslims, tested the potential of a cosmopolitan city outside the ancient walls. It was what sociologist Salim Tamari described as a hidden part of the city's history: "a late Ottoman and early Mandate Jerusalem, with a thriving nightlife and a considerable degree of intercommunal interaction and cultural hybridity."[17] Musrara is an integral part of this cosmopolitanism. Signs of modernity, for example, reached that district before others. The sewage system was brought to Musrara by the Ottomans in the nineteenth century. Electricity first arrived in the city in the large Notre Dame complex that acted as the divider between Musrara and the Old City and—from a political point of view—represented the strong presence of France, a Catholic power, before the arrival of the British Mandate.

Admittedly, electricity is not sufficient to define a community as modern. But Musrara was also home to experiments that cut heavily into the cultural and educational anachronisms of Jerusalem at the end of Ottoman influence. One example rises above all: The Dusturiyah, a school founded in 1909 by the prince of Palestinian pedagogy, Khalil al-Sakakini. Open to the different religious communities, with a ban on corporal punishment, open to a critical relationship between teachers and students, without examinations and homework, innovative and even revolutionary, the Sakakini school provided a secular alternative to the Ottoman mold of education. Even more than this, the Sakakini school was an alternative to the institutions opened by the ever more present foreign powers in Jerusalem. The Dusturiyah—the name means 'constitutional' in Arabic—is an example of Jerusalem's overlooked modernity, the secular modernity at the heart of the City of Three Faiths, above all in its openness to all religious communities, including Jews. "Among its students," writes Haim Hanegbi, a controversial figure of the Israeli Left and an exponent in the early 1970s of the movement of the Black Panthers in Jerusalem, "there were also some Jews, for example the children of the Mani, Moyal, and Amzaleg families, members of the old Sephardic Jewish community of Jerusalem."[18] Everyone could attend a school that would represent, for the Palestinian pedagogue, the expression of a city that contains cosmopolitan potential within its own composition and in its lines of communication with the sea (Jaffa) and the Syrian north (Damascus). Sakakini was only the most famous exponent of a Palestinian middle class that gave the city a precise imprint between the decadence of the Ottoman Empire and the arrival of the British.

Modernity is also the social life conjugated according to standards different from the communities' traditional social codes. It produces a neutral place where diverse groups of inhabitants could meet and interact with each other. Jerusalem's modern social life was not only found in the evening visits made by middle-class families with families of different faiths (Michel, for example, still remembers the smell of sesame oil in the house of his father's Jewish friend who had a shop on Jaffa Street). Concerts were also sites of modern socializing. Cafés and cabarets were concentrated between Musrara, Jaffa Street, and the Russian compound, serving as "the nodes where the Christian, Muslim, Jewish, and Armenian populations could interact, creating a confessionally shared space and neutralizing the diktat of social prohibitions."[19]

The microhistory of Musrara prior to 1948 has other protagonists: The Sephardic community, Jewish Ottoman citizens who in the decades up to the birth of the state of Israel had a relationship, sometimes excellent and sometimes tense, with Zionist immigration. Ironically, looking at the city from a post-Green Line perspective, Jews were concentrated in houses to the east of the 1948 armistice line. The Valeros, one of the most important Sephardic families in Palestine, owned not only a good part of the lands in the northern sector of the new city, in districts such as Mahane Yehuda and Romema, but also plots and commercial enterprises just outside Damascus Gate, where today Palestinian business is conducted in little shops and street vendors sell food in front of the ancient walls.[20]

The 'new city' in Jerusalem is therefore a composite. It was not just condensed into the area determined by rapid Zionist immigration. The Ottoman Palestinian 'little world' stepped out of the confines of the Old City, opened up before Zionist immigration, and then grew in parallel with the demographic and urban expansion of the new Jewish quarters of Jerusalem. It is the world of the Palestinian districts that is now to be found in the Jerusalem west of the Green Line. Before 1948, the development was primarily toward Lifta, in the north, in the direction of business, the railroad, new roads, and the sea. Now, Israeli real estate agents sell the Arab houses in Baq'a, Talbiyah, and Qatamun for high prices. Now, those houses and those neighborhoods are marked as west Jerusalem. Then—dozens of years before 1948, before 1967, before 1993—the development of the Palestinian bourgeoisie was concentrated in the west, attracted by Jaffa, by access to the sea, by the port of reference, by the passage along which goods and men would arrive. In that area it is still possible to glimpse Ottoman and Mandate Jerusalem through the porticos and the arched windows of the ground floors (on which three or four floors were built in successive decades).

Some say that Jerusalem was more lively and cosmopolitan then than it is today, now that it is the symbol of religious orthodoxy. Between the nineteenth and twentieth centuries, in fact, Jerusalem was a city in which ethnic divisions existed, and at the same time which provided a space for an urban way of living devoted to mixing. Jerusalem was a mélange: an Old City that closed its gates in the evening, and a new city that was emerging, composed not only of new areas of Jewish immigration but also of Palestinian areas that even today indicate some of the richer city neighborhoods.

When in 1948 the war divided the city, it also created a definition for the various parts of Jerusalem that contradicted the city's history and contemporary development: an Israeli west and a Palestinian east. As if from one or the other side of the Green Line nothing of the other communities existed. The Arab houses to the west of the armistice plan, however, are testimony that a diverse city really did exist.

Within Reach of the Snipers

Musrara was split in February 1949 by the war and the armistice plan supported by the international community. In the east, it lost its character as a district and was more or less reduced to a commercial street beginning at Damascus Gate and winding for dozens of meters to the north. A wall of three or four meters rose suddenly in front of this line of shops and workshops, protecting the Jordanian-administered part of the city. A few hundred meters divide the Palestinian from the Israeli part of Musrara. The heart of the district was dead, while in the stretch from one part to the other, known in Jerusalem by its English term, 'seam,' there were soldiers on guard and barriers to defend them from snipers. The western part of Musrara was essentially deserted, deprived of its inhabitants and of the bourgeois life that had characterized it since the first decades of its existence.

From 1948 and in the years until the conquest of the city by Israel in the 1967 war, even the ancient walls of Suleiman the Magnificent between Damascus Gate and New Gate were ramparts where Jordanian soldiers were posted. On the other side, in the big Notre Dame complex, there were Israeli soldiers. Barely a dozen meters separated the patrols that gazed across at each other for nineteen long years, during which the United Nations archives filled with denunciations of violations of the ceasefire from one side or the other. For nineteen years, there were only skirmishes and snipers reigning over a fragmented district.

The houses with the red tiles were not only abandoned; many were partially destroyed by grenades and the period of war. The houses no longer had the fascination they once had, left empty because of the sniper fire, while the little streets closer to no-man's-land were full of mines. No one from the west thought of going there to live, despite the scarcity of housing. Some, however, were willing to occupy what was left of Musrara. These were the families of Jewish immigrants from North Africa and the Middle East, forced to live in transit camps organized by Israel, primarily in the Negev. The waves of *olim*, new citizens, were too numerous, and it was difficult for a new state to satisfy the need for houses. The transit camps were not seen as transitory, the promised accommodation was late in arriving, and—tired of waiting—many of the Jews coming from the Arab world and from Iran, the *mizrahim*, decided to go to Musrara and other broken-down districts and to occupy the houses as squatters.

The lives of the new inhabitants of Musrara were very difficult. More than one of these inhabitants told me: "Here they used to shoot first. And we who lived there were cannon fodder on the borderline. In one room like this, ten of us were living in impossible conditions: cold in winter, hot in summer. There were hardly any schools and the children were always hungry." Others talked of the mines that made some areas of Musrara dangerous. Four or five families lived in the former houses of the well-off, often with only one communal bath and one makeshift kitchen. The sewers, built during the Ottoman period, had suffered the damages of war, as had all other utilities. This was a working-class suburb in the shadow of the walls of Suleiman the Magnificent.

Musrara's houses did not provide a solution to problems that only grew worse with time. The Israeli authorities, after a first attempt to block the settlement of the *mizrahim*, responded by building—hastily and cheaply—small working-class apartments, public housing similar to that which filled postwar Europe. These *shikunim*, the Israeli version of concrete working-class housing, arose on the outskirts of major cities. In Jerusalem, they were built in Qatamun, a wealthy Palestinian quarter that ended up west of the Green Line, and Musrara.

The new inhabitants of Musrara were part of the wave of immigration that between 1948 and 1964 brought some six hundred and fifty thousand new citizens to Israel. They were considered second-class citizens and gathered under one huge stereotype—'Moroccans.' The Israeli establishment, like some 85 percent of the Jewish population of Palestine in 1947–48, were Ashkenazi Jews coming mostly from Europe. The establishment did not comprehend the profound variation within the immigrant *mizrahim*: they had all come from the 'Orient' (hence the name) and they were not acculturated, not refined. They were not Europeans; whether they were Yemeni or Moroccan, whether they came from the great Jewish middle class of Cairo or Baghdad, made no difference. The Mizrahi question, in Israel, was born in the 1950s and became the subject of study, feeding an intellectual and social debate that continues today.

The Israeli state tried to forge a common national culture out of the melting pot, to erase the obvious differences among the diverse groups that made up its young society. "In practice, Ashkenazim could maintain their European identities (short of the Yiddish language and shtetl manners), but North African and Middle Eastern Jews were asked to suppress their culture while at the same time providing local flavor, token of food, dress, and music, thereby creating an indigenous link for a Middle Eastern nation conceived by European architects," writes Amy Horowitz, a scholar of popular Israeli culture. Thus, "Lebanese salad became Israeli salad, one example of the absorption of customs without differentiating among former group identities."[21]

Yet again, the microcosm of Musrara is exemplary. The quarter's *mizrahim* described their arrival and their life in Israel as marked by discrimination and also by an effort to keep their own ways of life while at the same time being recognized as Israelis on an equal level. The result is complex: a life on the brink between conservation and assimilation. Paradoxically, Musrara remained an 'Oriental' district even after the Palestinian flight of 1948, though its social life changed definitively from the Palestinian and Jewish middle class of the late Ottoman and Mandate periods to a new social group, poor and discriminated against. The post-1948 inhabitants of Musrara were new citizens of the state of Israel, though they shared with the middle-class Ottoman Sephardim an Arab-Jewish culture that distanced them from the Ashkenazi Israeli elite.

Musrara became a subproletarian urban district amid "the pungent odors of Moroccan food, coffee and spices," as noted by Roger Friedland and Richard Hecht, architects who came to study Musrara at the end of the 1970s. Friedland and Hecht, in their weighty study of Jerusalem, give a perfect description of the "Moroccan neighborhoods," of which Musrara is one.[22]

Many Jerusalemites steered clear of the Moroccan neighborhoods, fearing violent gangs, drug dealers, pickpockets, prostitutes, and the unattended children who seemed to roam there with no purpose except to make trouble. Despite years of community work, these neighborhoods remain central in the drug trade—heroin has replaced hashish as the primary narcotic on the local market. The 'Moroccan' kids who grow up tough, angry, and undisciplined fill Israeli prisons.[23]

In other words, the panorama of Musrara today is not a postcard. More than two thousand people live in six hundred and ten lodgings, often consisting of little more than one room. One-third survive on social benefits. There is overcrowding, degrading living conditions, and for children poor education. Dropping out of school is a normal practice, as is the delinquency of minors. Unemployment weighs heavily on males in traditionally conservative Sephardic families. Fathers work (or don't), mothers take care of the house, and there are many sons who often revolt.

Black Panthers in Musrara

Koko Deri has long criticized the Ashkenazi establishment. He was a member of the Black Panthers, the urban underclass movement that made Golda Meir's life difficult prior to the 1973 War. His attic apartment was opposite the armistice line, a hundred meters from Damascus Gate and Arab Jerusalem. It consisted of a twelve-square-meter room, a large terrace, and a tiny bathroom. The *panterim*, the Israeli version of the Black Panthers across the Atlantic, were born there in Deri's attic at the beginning of the 1970s. They shared with their American models a revolt against the establishment, in this case Ashkenazi, and self-pride. The *mizrahim* "have always been made to feel second class," as African-Americans were. They imported the logo of the Black Panthers, the closed fist that has appeared in rebellions the world over, reproduced in the graphics and posters of the Arab revolts of 2011, especially in nearby Egypt where it featured in the logo of the April 6 movement.

Deri jealously guards the memory of heroic times: the myth of the *panterim*. The young men of Musrara would gather in that attic facing the walls of the Old City. They would listen to music on an old transistor radio and smoke—that's all. In the beginning, these working-class boys were not political; they needed to pass the time somewhere other than on the streets. They were, however, truly street boys, marked as school dropouts with temporary jobs, some of the youngest from reformatories and on public assistance. They did not do military service because of their police records. They had nothing to do with the leftist militancy of certain members of the Israeli middle class or intelligentsia.

According to Deri, in a view that is not uncommon, "The paradox is that it was the far-leftist Ashkenazis who brought awareness of our situation. They convinced us to struggle against the Ashkenazi establishment to obtain more equitable living conditions." It was the "white" boys who would gather a hundred or so meters from Deri's attic who brought American protest myths to the attention of the "blacks." The Musrara boys, ranging in age from eighteen to twenty, became politicized in turn. They began going down to the square to ask for equality with the others. The leaflet distributed at their first demonstration reads: "We are demonstrating for the right to be considered equal to all the other citizens of our country." Their main request was to enjoy the rights they had been denied: the right to decent housing, thereby putting an end to the degrading districts; free education and housing for the needy; abolition of the authorities dealing with juvenile delinquency; salary increases for workers who support large families; and the final and most political request, full representation of "Eastern Jews" in all the country's institutions.[24]

From March 1971 on, the *panterim* held unauthorized demonstrations and marches, and employed the controversial tactic of stealing food in order to distribute it to the poor. More than anyone, they challenged one of the most important leaders in the country's history, Golda Meir. "They are not so nice," the 'Iron Lady' of Israeli politics famously said of the Israeli Black Panthers, a statement now carved on a plate affixed to a wall in Musrara to commemorate the movement. The *panterim*'s reply was voiced by Saadia Marciano, the movement's most charismatic member and an activist until his death of a tumor at age fifty-seven in 2007. "The cake is for everyone," said Marciano, whose boyish face became iconic, "or there will be no cake." The challenge to Meir and the Ashkenazi establishment was clear. At a demonstration in Zion Square, in the center of Jerusalem, protesters burned an effigy of the Israeli prime minister.

The *panterim*'s actions were above all symbolic. They stole milk from Rehavia, a well-to-do area of Jerusalem, and gave it to needy families, arguing that even cats had milk in Rehavia's houses, while in the Qatamun district's *shikunim* the babies lacked it. This was too much for the Israeli government, still in the hands of the Labor party and other left-wing parties. The leaders of the Black Panthers were arrested and put in administrative detention, demonstrations were repressed, and many protesters were injured and dozens imprisoned. The revolt continued throughout 1972, with its ups and downs, until it was buried on the day the new war began. Yom Kippur, 1973: the war Israel did not win, the war that continues to be the country's deepest psychological wound.

Although the *panterim* movement was not strong enough to withstand the 1973 War or the shift from a movement to a more structured organization, its cause did not end with the last of its demonstrations. It had not just been a boys' game. This is confirmed by the findings of a commission of inquiry into minors in poverty, the Horovitz Commission, ordered by Meir. The report underlined not only that the poorer economic sector consisted of "immigrants from Asia and Africa" but also that the government had no strategy to combat their distress. Not only had the *mizrahim*'s living conditions worsened during the 1960s, but, even more grievously, discrimination had grown in proportion with their level of education: the more they were educated, the more they were discriminated against.[25]

Perhaps historians will not agree with the reading of the Black Panthers given by Deri and his friends—Reuven Abergil, Marciano, Charlie Biton, and Kokhavi Shemesh, among others. "We have changed Israel," argued Deri. Certainly, the *panterim* were the Israeli face of the movements of the late 1960s that spread worldwide. They gave significance and dignity to a sociopolitical condition—that of the *mizra-him*—long hidden, despite the flames of protest lit some years previously, in the depressed Haifa neighborhood of Wadi Salib, where in 1959 the first effort was made to bring the Israeli government's attention to the needs of 'Eastern Jews.' Maybe because times changed, or maybe because the *panterim* emerged from the heart of Jerusalem, a revolt emerged from forgotten Musrara from 1971 to 1973. Even after becoming Jewish, Musrara left its mark on the history of Israel, if only because from the early 1970s the *mizrahim* became a constituency capable of influencing election results, of dictating conditions, and therefore of deciding who to send to government. With time, the *mizrahim* became one of the bases of the Israeli Right. They were the hard core on which Menachem Begin constructed his surprising victory in 1977, when for the first time the country participated in the defeat of the Labor party and enabled Likud's rise to power.

It is not therefore chance that one of Begin's first acts, just a month after the elections, was to launch an enormous project of reevaluating towns and neglected districts. Project Renewal was an ambitious plan that involved—at the financial level—the national government, munic-ipalities, and above all the Jewish diaspora. The plan was aimed at the hundreds of poor districts overwhelmingly inhabited by *mizrahim*, victims of a housing policy defined as "spatial enclosure," which "denote[d] the geographic segregation of the lower strata of [Israeli] society."[26] Begin's plan involved almost half a million people and a total cost of $2 billion, of which one-quarter was paid by the diaspora community through the Jewish Agency. In the first five years, starting in 1978, more than thirty thousand housing units were renovated. The national plan included Musrara, a district of little relevance from the point of view of number of inhabitants, but important for the image of Israeli—the Black Panthers' Musrara. This was how Begin compensated one of his important bases of support and at the same time confirmed that, under his government, there were truly two Israels. And thus the name of Menachem Begin, thirty years exactly after 1948, returned to Musrara, no longer reviled for the blood spilt in conflict but rather heralded for renovating the old houses of the district.

Musrara to the Musrarians

What happened in Musrara happened in many old town centers, for example in Europe, which were left to decay while large peripheries were developed. There was a very real economic interest in letting the district fall into decline. Those involved with Project Renewal spoke clearly: "There is evidence that the public authorities chose to allow Musrara to deteriorate because the long-run plans were to rebuild it as a small business district or more affluent neighborhood."[27] The plan was to drive the inhabitants to abandon the old Arab houses for a little apartment elsewhere, in which there would at least be a kitchen and a bathroom worthy of the name. The strategy worked for some inhabitants. The majority, however, did not want to leave Musrara. They had in mind the experience of another district near the walls of the Old City, Yemin Moshe. The neighborhood founded by Sir Moshe Montefiore had suffered a similar fate: its inhabitants, in exchange for their decaying lodgings, had received insignificant compensation, especially compared with what the district would become over the years. Yemin Moshe is now one of the most expensive and attractive places in Jerusalem.

Musrara's *mizrahim* did not leave the neighborhood. On the contrary, they fought to have a say in its renovation. The experts and benefactors who arrived to redevelop the area in fact tried not to impose any top-down town plan on the inhabitants. If there were to be renovations, they should be decided on by the residents, according to the principle of 'Musrara to the Musrarians,' even though community requests aroused some perplexity. The example that comes to everyone's mind is the story of the *mikveh*, a ritual bath. A *mikveh* was among the inhabitants' first requests, even before a synagogue. David Guggenheim, one of the architects invited to plan the restructuring of the district, interpreted the request as necessary because many of the houses lacked decent facilities. The ritual bath, he thought, came from a common and daily need, even greater than religion. Perhaps it was also a cultural necessity, seeing that almost all the inhabitants came from North Africa where the *hammam* served the double purpose of hygiene and a place to meet.

Dick Gunther, a successful contractor, presided over Project Renewal's national committee and served as the liaison between the Jewish community of Los Angeles that adopted Musrara through the Jewish Agency and the inhabitants of the tiny district of Jerusalem. For four years, he shuttled between the Pacific and the Mediterranean, clashing with a mentality that was not his, and with a group very removed from his usual surroundings. "Many of the people I have met must have spent certain periods in prison for having committed various crimes, nevertheless they were brilliant and obviously had the ability to manage successfully," he wrote in his memoirs.[28] Gunther had never made use of a *mikveh* in his life, nor had the other members of the committee, all secular Jews. The district's wish was respected, and obstacles, such as the need to ask a rabbi for permission to continue excavation after skeletons were found, were overcome. The *mikveh* location became one of the most important issues for the Musrara community. The choice landed on a one-story house that had belonged to the Ansari family prior to 1948 and had been hit several times during the war, once by a grenade. Yes, it was actually the house where Michel lived together with his family for ten years before fleeing in the April of 1948.

For Guggenheim, sitting in his office in the trendy German Colony neighborhood amid the papers on Musrara, jealously preserving the archives and records of a singular experience, Musrara represented a "unique urban weave that furnished a rich visual environment" and "evidence of the history and way of life in the Jerusalem of old times."[29] The renewal of Musrara—on which the Israeli authorities at the time imposed a Hebrew name, Morasha—was a human more than a professional experience. It involved the challenge of restoring the Arab houses and making them come to life again, but also an encounter with a close-knit but difficult constituency in the inhabitants of Musrara, an attempt to offer them a piece of a better and more beautiful world by means of architectural tools, and above all to offer them work, a future. Many of the inhabitants worked on the renovation project, hired by the contractors.

In Musrara, Begin's plan worked. The district became one of the trendiest places in Jerusalem. The renovated Arab houses—to which the *mizrahi* squatters obtained deeds through provisions in the Absentee Property Law, which took them from their original Palestinian owners— were passed from hand to hand. This is how Musrara changed its skin, as many of the squatters who had arrived and occupied the rubble of the district restored a house and secured its ownership, and then moved away. They sold the renovated houses for high prices and chose to go and live in brand-new apartment buildings far from the center of Jerusalem.

The Invasion of the Ultra-Orthodox

For a period, Musrara became again middle class and sought after, as it had been in the early years of its existence in the first half of the twentieth century. The Palestinian middle class was replaced by the Israeli intelligentsia, by the small international community made up of journalists, diplomats, United Nations officials, and, especially, artists. The new wave took the place of the pre-1948 Palestinians and the *mizrahim* who had given birth to the Black Panthers. It coincided with the Oslo interval, when many in Jerusalem believed in peace, in a two-state solution, in a city in which it was possible to cater for the different identities of its inhabitants. It was a brief period, no more than ten years—a golden age that would reunite Musrara's bourgeois origins with the new age. The Arab houses were transformed, levels added upon levels, upsetting the pre-1948 urban and architectural structure. The original 'skyline' was immortalized in a few old photos that show a long stretch of red tiled roofs on a square base.

Since then, Musrara has not resisted the thrust of the Israeli–Jewish orthodox that have arrived en masse in Jerusalem, searching not only for mystic inspiration but also for housing. In recent years, the French and Americans have joined in crowding out Musrara's secular intelligentsia, once again changing the customs of a quarter that for years was filled with the smells of Jewish–Moroccan cooking and now assumes the veils of orthodox Jewish women and a culinary mix that varies from Eastern European *cholent* to chicken broth. In the social housing of Musrara, small, anonymous gray three-story buildings, the *mizrahim* have been replaced by ultra-orthodox migrants from the nearby enclave of Mea Shearim. Musrara today is increasingly an appendix to the most orthodox district of the city, without any ties to its own past.

The Salesian convent and the kindergarten frequented by Palestinian children is a record of a different district. The property was returned to the Catholic Church after a long and difficult legal battle with the Israeli authorities, which had requisitioned it like they had other buildings. Now the Salesian convent is the emblem of a Christian presence in Musrara that stretches west to the great Russian compound and the Ethiopian Christian area, and east as far as the Dominican Bible School, the École Biblique.

On the other side of the old front, beyond Road No. 1, Arab Musrara never found a new identity—the identity of residents, of a community that lives in the district. Musrara on that side today is only a functional place, from businesses to logistics to transportation. The line of shops from Damascus Gate opens up into an area where all the delicacy of relations between Israelis and Palestinians is concentrated. These communities abut each other, almost touching yet ignoring the other, in those almost communal hours that end the Muslim Friday and begin the Jewish Sabbath. Ultra-orthodox families hurry through the streets leading from Mea Shearim to Damascus Gate. Busloads of Muslim pilgrims—Palestinian citizens of Israel for the most part—have just left the streets that encircle the part of the Old City close to the Dome of the Rock. Above, helicopters circle between Musrara and the Mount of Olives. It is as if the no-man's-land marked by Mandelbaum Gate, in front of the Mandelbaum House and serving as the passageway between east and west from 1948 to 1967, remains conjugated according to the vocabulary of a low-intensity conflict. The faithful of all the Religions of the Book brush by; international observers swarm among the little hotels and the religious centers; and Palestinians pack the terminal of the small buses that go to the Arab villages around Jerusalem, many of them cut off from Jerusalem since Israel built the Separation Wall in 2003. And, in the middle of everything, still on Road No. 1, the visible line that divides one Jerusalem from the other (settlers excluded): the tracks of the light rail. The light rail is the funereal monument for a city separated by peace and divided between two identities, recognizing the value of both. It unites Jewish Jerusalem, reaching as far as Pisgat Ze'ev, the settlement on the edge of Ramallah, and the Israeli settlements built to the east, in the part occupied in 1967, with Jaffa Street, still and always the commercial heart of the Jewish district.

Arab Musrara, like many parts of Palestinian Jerusalem, is today a remnant of what it used to be. It is more a gateway area and less a livable and cohesive neighborhood. But today's reality is itself only the footprint of a history in which there has been a sudden break. It is like a fossil buried in stone, following that same historical path of the two parts of Musrara: the Israeli part fully within the social changes of the country and the Palestinian part, frayed, no longer the soul of a time, without a new identity that could take the place of its ancient heritage. Arab Jerusalem is more and more split into tiny islands, compounds, enclaves, districts that have lost the necessary connection to city life. The reasons, of course, lie in the conflict. Most of all they can be found in the push for a 'united and undivided' Israeli Jerusalem, which has already distorted the city.

Jerusalem is now both the most populous Israeli city and the Palestinian city with the most inhabitants. Michel's 'memory lane,' however, is still there. With the accuracy of satellite technology, one need only go to Google Maps, put the cursor on the eastern Mediterranean, skim over the coast, and advance to Jerusalem. Position the cursor at the crossroads of Ha Ayin Het Street, where Moshe Dayan and Abdallah al-Tall drew the Green Line, to arrive at the end of the slope, as far as Shivtei Israel Street. According to these 'virtual' calculations, it spans exactly a hundred and ninety meters. Traveling in the real and complicated life of the City of Three Faiths, these hundred and ninety meters have become the regular passageway for those who have business in the city offices, the imposing complex built at the top of the hill in the 1990s. There exists, in fact, an ordinary, everyday city that sometimes follows a logic different from religious logic and sometimes uses the alibi of faith to cover the purely political. The rites of petty bureaucracy are mundane and territorial, because of which for example our little street has become a sort of transit area. Almost all the clients of Jerusalemite bureaucracy follow the same habits. They leave their cars down below in the parking lots on the main road, Road No. 1. Then they go up the hill, Israelis, Palestinians, employees, customers, residents, all of them walking slowly because the uphill trek is tiring. All are united by bureaucratic obligation: to pay the local house tax, register a document, or file a protest. Those hundred and ninety meters are one of the few stretches of Jerusalem in which east and west, Israeli and Palestinian, secular and orthodox may share not words but at least the piece of asphalt on which they walk. In a city united only by Israel's laws and not by a shared everyday life, a piece of asphalt is something. Those hundred and ninety meters are a sort of microcosm, a place where much of what happens in Jerusalem takes place.

For a few moments, the people on the sidewalk may observe the little world composed of a strange cocktail of social housing and old villas, bourgeois buildings and unlicensed structures. In recent years these have become the home of young ultra-orthodox families. Men and women come and go, children play, cars are parked. It is the to and fro of a district full of mothers and babies, for whom the rhythm of the week is regulated by religious practices, by prayers and daily studies, according to the strict division of duties between men and women, and above all by the obsessive respect for Shabbat. If it were not for this connotation, so strongly determined by orthodoxy, the daily activity would resemble that of any city. Then, the *sonderweg* of Jerusalem, its special and unique destiny—symbol of so many cities past, present, and future in strife—appears in the form of an Israeli police van. Police with submachine guns get out, stop four young Palestinian boys about fourteen years old, at most fifteen, and ask for their documents. A few too many words are exchanged, the kids scramble over a wall, and the least subservient one, his identity card checked by radio, is pushed into the van and driven away. His destination is likely two hundred meters further on, not even ten minutes on foot from the silent little street: the notorious Muskubiyah, the old Russian compound that through the course of history has changed both its owner and its purpose.

There in Musrara, Michel's memory lane remains, no more than five minutes on foot in an area that, practically speaking, is known only to someone who lives in the city, far from the eyes of tourists intent on following with precision the obligatory stages of their pilgrimage, who rarely look beyond the sacred stones. If they were to raise their eyes beyond the walls of the Old City, they would notice a small cluster of houses with red-tiled roofs, like a little village placed on a gentle slope.

2

ISLANDS IN THE FORTRESS

The city is a discourse, and this discourse is truly a language: the city speaks to its inhabitants, we speak our city, the city where we are, simply by living in it, by wandering through it, by looking at it.

—Roland Barthes[30]

The middle-aged lady was tall, elegant, and courteous, but also very tired. The work of an estate agent is repetitive, and tough: showing houses, becoming intimate with people, knocking on the doors of strangers who are in the middle of doing laundry and cooking sauce. Her face showed no embarrassment, however, when she took me to see a house in the north of Jerusalem. West Jerusalem. There was nothing attractive about the apartment—small cluttered rooms and shoddy furniture. But that apartment had one thing different from other apartments: a minaret. I could not believe my eyes: a private house built around a minaret, or, if you like, a minaret inserted into a private space, inside a house of Jewish Israelis.

I did not say anything. I thanked the kind estate agent and left, saying that the house did not suit me, and my family. I was embarrassed, but

39

I seemed to be the only one who was. That house betrayed a memory that seemed to have totally escaped the owners. A minaret signifies a mosque, a place of worship. And in some sectors of Jerusalem it implies a place of others. What was there before, around that minaret? The question remained in my mind, and it was a question about the memory of Jerusalem, or rather about the memories. It could sound redundant to say, but there are so many memories in Jerusalem, and with equal dignity, one with respect to the other. There is not just a Jewish or a Christian Jerusalem. There is an Arab, Muslim, Christian Jerusalem with its history, its houses, its mosques and its churches, its streets, its minarets. For almost seventy years, this is a city trapped by conflict, dragged by the coat strings from one part to the other.

The minaret surrounded by bedrooms and children's toys, the deconsecrated mosque, the place of worship transformed into a private house, all of those snapshots remained confined in a corner of my memory. Well hidden. And yet from time to time I went back to the neighborhood. Only to go shopping. Just a few hundred meters below the hill on which the minaret still stands lies a mall—a shopping center, or rather *the* shopping center of Jerusalem. The mall is absurdly ecumenical and open to all comers, in the name of consumerism, which does not look closely at who is buying or ask anyone for an identity card. At least it does not distinguish between the 'good' customers and the 'bad' ones, yet.

The Malcha mall, also known as Kanyon Yerushalayim, the "commercial center of Jerusalem," is precisely under the minaret of Malha, or Maliha. The name is more or less the same. Paradoxically, it has remained in Jerusalem's pop culture despite the conflict and international limbo in which the city lives. The name, only the name, survived the long-standing tension that has wrapped the city: The Malcha, the busiest mall in the city, takes its name from Malha, a Palestinian village partly destroyed by the 1948 war—Israel's war of independence, the Palestinian Nakba. Malha was an important part of the ring of villages that framed Jerusalem and formed its agricultural belt.

The minaret is still there, in a tranquil residential neighborhood that has nevertheless seen a significant increase in construction. Looming on the opposite hills are the huge buildings of the Holyland, a real estate project that led to the brief imprisonment of Jerusalem ex-mayor Uri Lupolianski, together with a partner in former Israeli Prime Minister Ehud Olmert's legal firm. Indeed, the Holyland project involved Olmert in the most awkward affair of his political career. The red flowers on the hibiscus bushes surrounding the little garden by the minaret are in bloom. At the top of the minaret, which bears all the marks of time, bends a bronze crescent. The highest stonework is broken. The only nod to modernity is a strange jerry-rigged radio antenna attached to the minaret. The house is now inhabited by secular Israelis. Shabbat makes everything loose and relaxed. And the minaret is like a fixed image amid ongoing life.

In time I learned something more about that minaret. It belonged to the Palestinian village mosque. It belonged to Malha's mosque. Umm Adnan had the impudence of the young when she climbed it as a child to admire a panorama of terraced sloping land and hills that followed one after the other. Her large family lived in Malha and worked the land around the village. They used to take the vegetables, fruit, and milk to the markets in Jerusalem on foot. One of her uncles even succeeded in getting a good job at the YMCA, the sports, cultural, and religious inter-national center built right in front of the King David Hotel during the British Mandate, inside the middle-class 'new Jerusalem.' Umm Adnan, a Palestinian girl from Malha, had to escape with her family in April 1948, when horrific news reached them. The Irgun had perpetrated a massacre in Deir Yassin, only a short distance from Malha. Umm Adnan's family took refuge first in the countryside, under the trees, in the vicinity of Bethlehem, and then in East Jerusalem. Now, Umm Adnan, who was already ill when I met her, rests in peace. *Allah yirhamha.*

City Surrounded by Walls

The best spot is at the end of the right aisle, near the choir. From the benches near the chapel, there is a perfect view of the apse's marvelous mosaic in Santa Maria in Trastevere in Rome, Italy. Over the walled and turreted city in the mosaic the writing says "Hierusalem." From the colored and golden turreted Jerusalem six of the twelve apostolic lambs leave, drawn toward the center by the Agnus Dei, like a magnet. It is from the other end of the mosaic, dating from about 1140, where Bethlehem is portrayed, that the other six lambs leave for the same destination. Since then, Jerusalem and Bethlehem have been considered part of the same story, spiritually and—certainly—geographically, as Fr. Michele Piccirillo explained in a 2005 article, denouncing the idea of the separation of the two cities by a wall of concrete. "In the mosaics that decorate the triumphal arches of Rome's churches," wrote Piccirillo, "early Christianity's artists represented the two vignettes of Bethlehem and Jerusalem together as a symbol of the church of the pagans and of the church of the circumcision. Through Bethlehem and Jerusalem, they indicated the Church spreading all over the world as composed of pagan Gentiles and Jews. A unity that politics has nowadays the intention of splitting up, separating families and a centuries-old history that is not easily eradicated."[31]

A turreted city, surrounded by walls, that is, a sheltered city. In one of Rome's most beautiful basilicas, amid the cloud of incense, Jerusalem appears as it still is today, with walls and turrets. Concrete walls and watchtowers are certainly different from the walls and turrets depicted during the Byzantine period in the twelfth-century Trastevere mosaic and—in earlier times—in the most complete and important mosaic of its period, the sixth-century map of Madaba. Yet, still, a caged city.

The Holy City was represented as an architectural and religious pearl enclosed in a shell of walls. And as a fortified city it was preserved, despite the vicissitudes experienced by Jerusalem over the centuries—invasions, crusades, and destruction. In contemporary times, Sir Ronald Storrs, the first British military governor of the city after the defeat of the Ottoman army in 1917, led Jerusalem along the same lines and issued a direct order forbidding by ordinance "the demolition, construction, alteration or repair of any building in Jerusalem" in order to "protect" the city, "preserving the esthetic 'status quo', and the status quo in regard to religious worship and political status."[32] This was not Storrs's philological obsession. If anything it was an effort to modernize what he—the son of an Anglican priest—had assimilated in his religious consciousness, regardless of whether it was accurate to the urban reality of the Levant or part of an orientalist and biblical mythicization. It was necessary to preserve as an open-air museum what the Holy Land was to the small groups of nineteenth-century travelers: a list of biblical places traced in contemporary

Palestine. As a governor and a believer, Storrs wanted to preserve the Holy Land, and finally to protect turreted Jerusalem. He "sought to preserve the silhouette of a city encircled by a wall and towers, with domes and turrets soaring overhead, surrounded by olive groves,"[33] remarked Meron Benvenisti, vice mayor of Jerusalem under Teddy Kollek.

Storrs's vision, in short, was as mythical as that of Hierusalem inscribed in the splendid mosaic of Trastevere. Yet, in his aesthetic conception of the sanctity of Jerusalem, Storrs also gathered the fact that the city should be treated as a delicate, fragile object. A crystal glass. This idea is the source of a somewhat artificial regulation by which the British would be remembered among the rulers of the city. Jerusalem must continue to be built in stone, even outside the Old City. In what is generically considered 'new Jerusalem' anything is allowed from an architectural point of view, but it has to be covered with the white stone of Jerusalem. This artificial and out-of-date regulation of the Mandate era is today like a safe-conduct document, or like a Band-Aid applied to a wound, to hide it from sight. Buildings of uncertain taste spring up in West Jerusalem, and the profusion of cement gives an even more rigid exterior to a Spartan residential architecture that almost always retains nothing oriental in a forest of square windows, small balconies, and dull gray metal. The façade, however, is always spared: covered with stone.

The white stone also covers any kind of construction on the other side of Jerusalem, east of the Green Line. In the Palestinian sector buildings rise without a license, which is more or less impossible to obtain from Israeli authorities. At least the stone of Jerusalem is there to cover everything, turning Jerusalem into an apparently homogenous city, albeit a rather pale one. It is a pallor that points to sickness. Jerusalem is no longer ancient but it is old.

Once, by contrast, Jerusalem and the Old City were the same overlapping urban space. The first thing that groups of travelers noticed throughout the centuries of pilgrimage to the Holy Land were the sixteenth-century walls of Suleiman the Magnificent, the towers, the domes. That is no longer the case. Jerusalem is no longer a small provincial city surrounded by a wall, as it was until the Ottoman period, light years away from the great centers where politics and culture reigned in the Levant.

Damascus, Aleppo, Baghdad, Beirut. It has become a densely populated and extensive city, the biggest city in Israel. This kind of transformation—from a totally provincial urban center into the internationally unrecognized capital of Israel—originated with the Israeli–Palestinian conflict. Without the necessity of controlling the city, its borders and its demographics, there probably would not have been such rapid expansion. To put this in context, Jerusalem's population at the end of 2014 consisted of nearly nine hundred thousand Israelis and Palestinians, nearly double the population from 1983.[34]

In Jerusalem's new configuration, thus, the Old City is no longer *the city* in its entirety, as it was for centuries, when the urban space was completely enclosed by its ancient walls. The Old City is nowadays more than ever Jerusalem's heart, filled with temples, holy places, shops, tension, and outbursts of violence. The city walls are hidden within a much more complex and broader urban composition, as is common in each and every contemporary metropolis. The old historical center is compressed by the overwhelming peripheries. The paradox of history, however, requires that even today, almost a century and a half after European pilgrims' Grand Tour, Jerusalem appears to travelers to be a fortified city. Jerusalem is still a city within walls, that is, the archetype of an antimodern city. The ancient walls of Suleiman the Magnificent contain 'only' the religious and tourist dimensions of one of the most contested places in the world. Instead, third millennium Jerusalem is enclosed by the Wall, a concrete wall of separation to the Palestinians and a 'defensive barrier' to the Israelis. As a newly equipped fortress, Jerusalem is now caged inside a security system composed of the Wall and checkpoints, guarded entrances, terminals—postmodern drawbridges.

After a period of openness to modernity, between the end of the Ottoman Empire and the beginning of the British Mandate, during which construction began outside the walls and gates, Jerusalem has returned to its premodern state. The city, once again, surrounds itself with a wall, an even higher wall made of cement. As happened in 1873, it has even closed the gates that lead into the city, for protection from the outside. The most recent and postmodern wall is the one constructed by Israel over the last dozen years: reinforced concrete that penetrates the city, cuts out Lazarus's Tomb, and stretches for almost one and a half kilometers as the crow flies from the ancient walls, winding like a snake and enclosing al-Quds University, the Palestinian university of Jerusalem, led for twenty years by Sari Nusseibeh and now under the presidency of Imad Abu Kishek. To the south, the cement barrier separates the city from what for centuries was its appendix, Bethlehem, enclosed today as in a gray and imposing cul-de-sac, a snake of concrete that divides and tears the familiar fabric of the Palestinian population. It actually happens, and is not uncommon, that a husband is on one side of the Wall and his wife is on the other. The children must remain with one of the parents, according to the identity document in their possession, or the family remains united because one of the parents is living clandestinely, in order to remain with their partner and children.

The Wall is seen differently by the travelers, residents, and inhabitants: the prefabricated slabs of cement as high as nine meters, the barbed wire, and then the terminals, the security gates that lead into the city from all the cardinal points. The so-called checkpoints are more than just temporary police blocks; they are true and actual border passages, which incidentally have often been built on Palestinian territory.

Travelers driving from the airport in Tel Aviv to Jerusalem clearly understand that the paradigm has not changed: Jerusalem is still a fortress, on par with a medieval castle. The asphalt corridor of Route 443 leading to Jerusalem passes through the West Bank, but Palestinians are allowed to use it for only about thirty kilometers, half the distance between the airport and the Holy City. It is a highway channeled into a corridor bounded by walls or barbed wire to the left and right. A memory suddenly comes to mind. It happened once in pre-1989 Berlin. It was the journey from Hamburg to West Berlin, passing through hundreds of kilometers of East Germany on a train that did not stop at the stations, rushing through them, as if the panorama were simply a nightmarish backdrop. It was a closed train that arrived in the evening in a city, Berlin, lit up at night between track, railroad switches, and walls. End of journey. *Willkommen*, welcome to the island.

Welcome to the island-fortress of Jerusalem. Or rather, welcome to the archipelago, made up of islands and enclaves, that is, places of the powerful that communicate with the rest of the world and unconnected enclaves of the powerless that, on the contrary, communicate with the outside only with permission or prohibition by whoever administers the space. Similar to tourist resorts or 'green zones' in cities such as Baghdad or Kabul, the space of the powerful in Jerusalem is a closed and protected space. For example, an Israeli inhabitant of Jerusalem can easily reach Tel Aviv, the airport, and the sea. A Palestinian who lives in a district of East Jerusalem, Isawiya, or Abu Tor might suddenly and without any warning find the road between his district and the city closed by a police checkpoint, and could be denied access to the rest of Jerusalem. The antinomy between 'archipelago' and 'enclave' is what was described precisely by architect and researcher in urbanism Alessandro Petti. Petti calls the archipelago "the smooth space of flows," while the enclave is "the spaces of the exception." Petti explains: "The archipelago can accommodate both legal and illegal flows inside its space, whereas enclaves have no type of connection: they are isolated by some kind of power that may be internal or external to them, a power they submit to or which they exert. There is a substantial difference between being enclosed and enclosing oneself: it is what distinguishes a concentration camp from a luxury community."[35]

Third millennium Jerusalem has contradictory spatial and social urban elements. There is an archipelago of islands connected with each other internally and with external space, and a parallel set of enclaves, controlled by whoever administers the city. Jerusalem as an urban space is closed to the outside by checkpoints, *machsom* in Hebrew. Palestinians have incorporated the same word in their daily language. The checkpoints are Jerusalem's postmodern drawbridges, which allow entry into Jerusalem or, if they are—relentlessly—raised, prevent access to the city.

Coffee and Cigarettes at the Checkpoint

Bethlehem wakes up early. Like Jerusalem. They are Spartan cities where, for centuries, the relationship with the land has marked the times of day. In recent years, however, the wake-up call in Bethlehem sounds earlier than usual, in an unreal time deep in the night, for whoever has to go to work in Jerusalem. The clock may strike two or maybe three in the morning precisely when the troops of commuters set off from Bethlehem, from

Beit Jala, from Beit Sahour, from the whole belt of villages around the place venerated by Christians as the birthplace of Jesus. Late at night, the troops of commuters begin to move together toward the Wall. This is where those who hold the green identity card, or *hawiya*, issued by the Israeli authorities to Palestinians living in the Occupied Territories, and not in Jerusalem, must go. Difference among Palestinians starts with a color. The identity document of those who reside in the West Bank and Gaza is green, and occasionally but rarely orange. Blue, the most desirable, is the *hawiya* of the Palestinians who reside in Jerusalem. They are the Palestinian Jerusalemites, and not of the *tamanya wa arba'in*, the 'forty-eights,' those Palestinians who hold Israeli citizenship and belong to the Arab minority that remained in 1948 in the portion of land that became Israel. About three hundred thousand Palestinians who reside permanently in East Jerusalem hold the blue ID, and can move around fairly easily in Israel, in the West Bank, but not in Gaza. They are in a strange limbo, those with a blue ID, a little document contained in a blue plastic cover: they have no passport, they are not citizens, but in recompense they can call themselves Jerusalemites. They are from Jerusalem. They have the right to social services, to the hospitals, to move around the city, and to go to the schools.

"Sometimes we are ashamed of having this blue-colored *hawiya*," says Muna, nervously smoking a cigarette, as the group of young girls from East Jerusalem around her nod their heads to emphasize a common sentiment. "It is as if I am privileged if I enjoy the freedom that my friends beyond the Wall, in Bethlehem or Ramallah, will never have." "But what freedom?" echoes Rasha, who is a little older than twenty. "Our movements are never free. It is as if we live in a slightly larger enclosure than the others, but our freedom is just as much under surveillance!"

Palestinians are under surveillance, for example, when they go to pray in the Old City, especially Palestinian Muslims. For many years, and continuing until today, access to the Noble Sanctuary, the Haram al-Sharif, has been strictly limited for security reasons. On Fridays, Israeli authorities have enforced age restrictions on men willing to go and pray in the Old City, gradually forbidding access, first, to those under the age of forty, then those under forty-five, and, in the most recent years, those even under fifty. Palestinian youth who are not allowed to pass through Damascus Gate or Lions Gate perform the rite of prayer on the sidewalks right outside the Old City and in front of the Israeli soldiers. It is both a political and a religious ritual, the prayer carpets—carried as usual on shoulders—are ostentatiously placed on the ground. And in parallel to the great prayer at al-Aqsa, the youth carry out the rites, the five positions of the *salah*, they kneel, they stand, their arms folded on their chests. Thus they denounce the limitations that prevent the Palestinian Muslim faithful from reaching their sacred places to worship.

Compared to their male companions, East Jerusalem's girls are a little freer, but not much. Yet, Jerusalemites' freedom under surveillance seems an unattainable goal for their friends in Bethlehem who, in the deep of night, leave home with their identity card contained in a little purse identical to the one carried by the girls of East Jerusalem, except for its color: green instead of blue. And the world, seen through green lenses, changes totally. They wake up in the middle of the night, well before the dawn call to prayer. When the *fajr* melody raises up, the male companions of Muna and Rasha are already in line, herded like sheep in the long corridor that leads to the Bethlehem terminal, controlled by Israeli security personnel, soldiers, or even private guards. It is the main entrance, the drawbridge that leads into Jerusalem across a fortified cement wall, nine meters high.

Funneled and crowded, like a flock of sheep, in a corridor enclosed by a metal railing, men of all ages line up to go to work. In their hands they have the green *hawiya*, the work permit, and the unfailing cup of coffee, often together with a cigarette. There is no need to bring coffee from home, and the cigarette could be left behind at home on the bedside table. Inevitably a *suq* appears spontaneously near all the important gates that lead to Jerusalem. Informal markets grow suddenly near terminals, checkpoints, *machsomim*, crossings according to the incomprehensible 'controlled chaos' that is born of demand. And sellers offer what the commuters need: coffee, cigarettes, bread, and a small bag of *zaatar*, eggs, pitas.

If the terminal is the postmodern version of a drawbridge, then life continues beside it—just as it used to be along the walls of medieval castles. Wherever there is a crowd, there is a need and there is trade. Checkpoints' informal markets diversify their merchandise according to the season. From pyramids of strawberries exposed to car and truck exhaust fumes to chickpeas in their pods; from almonds in the spring, still wrapped in their damp husks, to *mishmish* or the apricots at the end of May. And then grapes, bananas, cellular phones, SIM cards, flowers, mechanical spare parts, fresh fruit juice. The informal markets are super-markets in the shadow of a fortified cement wall, military jeeps, and the turrets of the Israeli armed forces that control everything.

Seen from a distance, on foot or rolling down the car window, the Qalandya terminal that leads from the northern side of Jerusalem toward Ramallah looks like a mad undisciplined anthill, where driving on the wrong side of the road or passing over a roundabout could be considered the result of hysteria and of damned haste. It is not like this. Qalandya has its own unwritten, silent rules to channel a precariousness that has become permanent over the years.[36]

Observing Qalandya is enough to understand that this particular circle of hell follows a precise order to which everyone pays attention. If there is traffic along the route leading to the terminal, if the line of cars and minibuses begins well before the Wall, it sparks reflections on the reasons for the line. And drivers try alternative plans. The local radio and phone calls to relatives and friends can help to settle the logistics of a route through minor checkpoints in the countryside that is never either simple or usual. Has there been an accident? Are there protests? Clashes at Qalandya are recurring. Stone-throwing by Palestinian youth is met with teargas, rubber bullets, or even—ever more frequently—live ammu-nition from Israeli soldiers. Thus, the 'controlled chaos' of Qalandya may suddenly vanish into a real and tragic battleground 'organized' into two fronts: one made up of Palestinian youths on the main street and the other, closer to the Wall, where the Israeli soldiers are on guard. In the middle, burnt tires, trash carts, improvised obstacles. The smoke of tear-gas hangs over everything.

At that point Qalandya becomes an off-limits zone for commuters and for all those who need to pass through. No one among the workers and the regulars at the checkpoint objects to the youth's resistance, how-ever. No one at Qalandya protests at being forced to find an alternative route into Jerusalem. In a kind of addiction to the paradigms of conflict, the commuters take note of the unexpected closure of the entrance and begin to scour the countryside of the West Bank, street by little street, sometimes familiar to the driver and sometimes taken by intuition or directions from a passerby. Long circumnavigations of tens of tiring kilometers are often met with irrepressible sarcasm, the typical Palestinian humor that exorcizes the difficulty of daily living.

If, on the other hand, Qalandya is open, and the traffic is, so to speak, normal, the commuters get ready for the crossing. This means confronting the humiliating traffic jam of cars and minibuses that throng as in a comic strip. Above all, they get prepared for the psychodrama they will have to experience in presenting the required documents that allow them to go 'over there,' to Jerusalem. Qalandya life revolves around the commuters who are returning home to the City of Three Faiths or around those, far fewer these days, who have permission to enter: the poorest boys of the nearby refugee camp who sell whatever they can, from chewing gum to Kleenex tissues; the fathers hurrying to do a little shopping at the stalls before returning home; the students, always on foot as is the habit in Jerusalem, who dive in and out of the vehicles, despite the dust and asphalt, making their way home. Qalandya functions as an expressway, a chaotic market, a highway intersection, a tollgate, a square, a theater, an open-air prison. Marc Augé might well insert Qalandya and the areas around other checkpoints into the catalog of 'non-places' for which the French ethno-anthropologist has become famous.[37] Qalandya and the checkpoints are similar to classic non-places—stations, airports, supermarkets, highways, inns—places for a temporary halt, postmodern caravanserais, bounded transit sites where activity is in some ways covered by anonymity, where interactions are promiscuous, where one is one among many. Everybody is anonymous, but certainly only until the true and proper terminal is reached.

As far as the Qalandya and Bethlehem crossings are concerned, the architectural concept has to be as reassuring as it can be. The checkpoints that control the route through the Separation Wall thus resemble a normal highway tollbooth, except for the well-armed soldiers controlling the passage of vehicles and pedestrians. Aseptic and sterile as an airport terminal or a highway toll booth, the drawbridges that regulate

the entrance to Jerusalem have to not convey a sense of chaos and inse-
curity. It is as if between the terminal and the indescribable traffic jam in
the area beside the Wall there is a transparent screen that further defines
a 'here' and a 'there.'

The description of Hagar Kotef and Merav Amir, two Israeli women
activists belonging to the Machsom Watch rights association, tells us a lot
about the indissoluble relationship among the form of the checkpoints,
their value, and their significance.

> They are built like border crossings, reinforcing the illusion that
> they are normal sites marking the border between two sovereign
> entities and concealing the fact that Israeli rule applies on both
> sides of the terminal. With seemingly friendly welcome signs,
> vast parking lots (in which no one parks—the Palestinians have
> no access by car to the checkpoint area), benches (on which no
> one sits), toilets (which are often out of order), the terminals
> present a facade of legitimacy.[38]

It does not matter that only one of the two parties in conflict—in this
case Israel—determines the rules for entering Jerusalem, and above all
encloses the city like a castle. The legitimacy derives from the Israeli
state, from the necessity of security for its citizens, from the affirmation
that Jerusalem "is the unique and indivisible capital of Israel." The rest,
all the rest, will be discussed one day. For the time being in the city-fortress 'of peace,' people have access by way of drawbridges that at a certain
hour of the evening are closed, because even the checkpoints, the gates of
the Wall, and Qalandya itself seem to go to sleep as well.

Daily Non-places

It is a short step from the Bethlehem checkpoint to Mega. It is a short
stroll from the Separation Wall at Bethlehem to the most secular and
popular supermarket of Jerusalem, two kilometers at most. Yet the distance between the checkpoint and the supermarket is abysmal, even
though both might be defined by a different measure as non-places. The
checkpoint epitomizes the non-place that has been built for sorting the

good from the bad in the group, whereas the supermarket as a non-place contains everything and everybody, at least from the spatial point of view. But be careful not to be charmed by the idea that the supermarket, the grand department store, could be the solution to the ills of Jerusalem and represent the reconciled 'common space.' In this sense Augé is right: "The space of non-place creates neither a single identity nor relations; only solitude and similitude."[39]

It is not an inconsequential detail from a Jerusalemite perspective if everyone in Mega, Israeli and Palestinian, shares the aisles and lines at the cash register, spending time side by side, brushing against each other, possibly, looking at each other. They are together in a supermarket that differs in no way from any of the big supermarket chains all over the world: shelves, lots of shampoos and coffee, a profusion of greens from Israeli hothouses. If anything, the difference, as far as western societies are concerned, is in the products' packaging and size. Single doses or single quantities are almost nonexistent. Products have to meet the needs of large families: shampoo, bubble bath, cornflakes, milk, everything is extra-large, more like the American than the European consumerism model. And Mega wins, because the same products cost less, compared to other supermarkets in Jerusalem. Low prices are a good reason for everyone, Israelis and Palestinians alike, to go up and down the aisles, because there is never enough money at the end of the month and crisis bites even in Jerusalem—a city where poor people are clearly visible.

Mega, the supermarket, the non-place, is therefore a space where it is possible to see the city's inhabitants all together. Together as strollers and consumers, not as inhabitants: at Talpyot people do not live together. Instead, Talpyot is where Jerusalemites of all sorts go shopping. It is a strange kind of open-air mall that begins from West Jerusalem's rich periphery and reaches the southern offshoots of the city, between the large settlement of Har Homa and the Wall that separates it from Bethlehem. Talpyot is a commercial magnet, because the prices are competitive, the offerings are attractive, the choice very abundant. And then there is everything, from the Israeli do-it-yourself furniture factory to the Japanese and European car dealers, even the office that issues the obligatory environmental compliance certificate for a car.

At first sight nothing seems to have changed since ancient times, in which markets were the meeting place, where everyone went to get provisions. Also the atmosphere is relaxed at Mega, the postmodern version of the *suq*. A large cross-section of customers frequents the supermarket: there are petty bourgeoisie and working-class people, and even some intellectuals who avoid the nearby German colony neighborhood and its gentrified ambiance. The butcher is Palestinian, the cashier wears the hat of moderately orthodox Jewish women. "The prices here are the best in the city," said Iman, a middle-aged Palestinian Christian woman. Mega is an obligatory stop for her on her journeys to and fro between Jerusalem and Bethlehem. "Also, the environment isn't hostile." Translated: there is no friction between Israelis and Palestinians.

Just as paradoxically, there is no friction along Jaffa Street, the scene of some of the bloodiest terrorist attacks that shook the city in the second half of the 1990s and during the Second Intifada. There, in the commercial heart of West Jerusalem, a short stroll from the Old City, Palestinians and orthodox Israelis are united in one common objective: buy clothes, shoes, shirts, and coats at much lower prices. And low prices matter, for very large and poor families, especially when presents must be bought for the required feasts, such as Eid al-Fitr for Muslims, which ends the sacred fasting month of Ramadan, or Sukkot for Jews, which is the Feast of Tabernacles.

Does the path of peace go through the market? Too lovely, and too simple, to be true: Jerusalem is a place where identity and land go arm in arm. History did not have to expect the unrest that Jerusalem experienced in June 2014, after four young Israelis were kidnapped and killed by Palestinians near the illegal Israeli settlements in the Hebron area. After the news spread, Jaffa Street experienced days and nights of the first 'civil war' unrest. Israeli youth chased Palestinian teenagers, chanting, "Death to the Arabs," even trying to lynch them. Palestinian residential areas such as Beit Hanina experienced not only clashes between Palestinian youth and Israeli police, but also the abduction of a sixteen-year-old student, Muhammad Abu Khdeir, who was killed and burned by Jewish extremists.

Seeds of a profound change in Jerusalemites' attitude between communities sprouted especially in recent years, following the shift in the demographic balance toward a more significant presence of radical religious settlers in the city. Research carried out in 2010 by the Floersheimer Institute of the Hebrew University of Jerusalem under Marik Shtern established that many Israelis were annoyed by the presence of Palestinians in commercial areas, in large department stores, in markets. Discomfort, fear, alienation were the feelings described by the interviewees when they found themselves in common spaces.

Malcha Mall is the common space par excellence. Or rather the Kanyon, as it is called by the inhabitants of Jerusalem, using the Hebrew term, thus overcoming even the linguistic barriers. A strange melting pot is the order of the day, at Kanyon. The king of the malls in Jerusalem, on three levels, it accommodates medium-size and large self-service shops, office equipment retailers, supermarkets, toy shops, and coffee bars. There is also a cinema for all ages. It is enough to attract people from the suburbs, either Palestinians who cannot find the same product in East Jerusalem or Israelis. What makes the Kanyon special is that truly everyone is used to going there, from secular to orthodox, from hairstyling-gel youth to big families with lots of children, whether Muslim or Jewish. And for the merchants, consensus that unites the communities around consumerism is all gold that sparkles. Business is good, and customers don't refuse consumers, as I witnessed at the time of writing. Even a good segment of employees working in the coffee bars, shops, and supermarkets is Palestinian.

However, the Kanyon's consensus has nothing to do with politics. Because the serious questions go well beyond wedding presents or shoes for children. Land is land. An unwritten truce is accepted at the mall. Just outside, a few kilometers away, it is a completely different story. Stones fly, and teargas also. And yet, although the unwritten truce in the commercial center does not in any way intrude on the political destinies of the city, the contrary is true. Malcha Mall is an important element in the actual Jerusalemite pattern. It does not only represent parentheses in a daily life imbued with an enduring conflict. Nor does it only represent a breath of fresh (or more precisely, air-conditioned) air in a day permeated by constant tensions. In many ways it fulfills the function of no-man's-land beyond the political dimension and completely within the social dimension. In a singular way, the mall satisfies the need for a truce. It is the brief ceasefire in a Jerusalem day described by Zygmunt Bauman in a perfect synthesis: "Shopping malls make the world (or the carefully walled-off, electronically monitored and closely guarded part of it) safe for life-as-strolling."[40]

In the city pilgrims yearn for most, the true place of peace (or at least non-belligerence) is to be found not in the shade of temples or in the sacred places within the Old City but rather in a large shopping mall controlled under the gaze of guards that monitor the entrances and security. The walled-off mall facilitates the truce in the form of strolling, wandering, brushing against each other. These kinds of parentheses amid the daily conflict of Jerusalem do not touch identities, but at the same time they stress that Israelis and Palestinians, secular and orthodox, enemies and adversaries share the single identity of consumers. Consumerism and its liquid modernity, however, do not succeed in crumbling the solid structure of belonging to a community, a people, a culture, and a faith.

The detour to Malcha Mall or the Mega supermarket, or the window-shopping in Jaffa Street or the new Mamilla open-air mall, is perceived by Jerusalemites as necessary to preventing madness. It is almost the equivalent of a prison's yard time, because strollers and consumers consider these actions as they are: not reality, nor life. Malls are fake neutral spaces (entrances are controlled by Israeli security guards, for example), where there may possibly be dispensations of the respective communities' social codes. Look at the behavior of the coffee bar waiters or the shop employees! It is even possible to joke, as when a Palestinian waiter manages to tease his female Israeli colleague by putting an ice cube down her sweater. A delicate gesture, full of modesty, and at the same time risky, that is greeted by the young woman with a scream, without any resentment, if anything amusement. Such a scene anywhere in Europe, perhaps almost in any other place in the world, would be just a little scene. Such jokes in the workplace would not rouse any curiosity or be important enough to be filed away in an observer's memory. However, in Jerusalem it becomes a revolutionary scene, an exception with two possibilities: that the exception confirms the social conformity of the city, or that the exception sows a seed of real hope, without rhetorical tricks. The real hope may lie in the interactions among those who work at the mall, and not among the consumers, or, as Walter Benjamin would say, the *flaneur*.[41]

Among the workers, therefore, it becomes apparent how much of a digression the mall really is, a respite, a breath of fresh air in the conflict. It is because the codification of behavior is different: they put on the uniforms of waiters, and they behave differently, they recognize each other as (almost) equal, speak to each other, joke and accept the joke. Then off with the uniform, out of the gates, and back to their own very homogenous quarters, where a community of a single kind lives. The mall can be a fixed-term oasis, at least until a bunch of hooligans come to break up the strange, artificial harmony.

The presumably happy island of Malcha Mall is nevertheless an island. It is an enclosed space beyond which the real city lives. Beyond the department store's area there is the old Palestinian village of Maliha, now an Israeli residential zone. Among the traces of the village is the old minaret that Umm Adnan climbed when she was a child. Facing the mall, just in front of the highway that runs along the parking lot, there is a place that represents the opposite of consumerism's intermingling. Jerusalem's football stadium, dedicated to Teddy Kollek, is a place that over the years has become a symbol of racism, through the shouts of soccer hooligans.

This icon of racism has a name: Beitar Yerushalayim, the historical Israeli team of Jerusalem. In the spring of 2012, Beitar Yerushalayim's hooligans made their first 'small' raid on Malcha Mall, picking on the Palestinians who were working or shopping there. It was not a big deal: the stadium and the mall are exactly face to face. Beitar Yerushalayim's fans are known not only for a generic racism but also for a specific anti-Arab coloring. Not a single Palestinian player has ever joined the Beitar team, whereas Palestinians play in Haifa's Maccabi and especially in Bnei Sakhnin, to mention just two well-known Israeli teams. Not all of Beitar's fans, supposedly as many as a million people in the whole of Israel, are of course racists, but it is a matter of record that for decades the supporters have been known for, and sometimes imposed to the extreme, anti-Arab racism. The team's history fits completely with that of the Zionist rightist faction even prior to the birth of the state of Israel. Beitar symbolized Ze'ev Jabotinski's revisionist youth movement, as opposed to the other Jerusalem team, Hapoel, which was an offshoot of the most important Jewish union, the Histadrut. Until 1991, when the Teddy Kollek Stadium opened, Beitar Yerushalayim trained and played at the YMCA, the sports and cultural center built in front of King David Hotel, one of the rare signs even today of spatial sharing among the three religious communities, who play basketball together, go to the swimming pool, and frequent the kindergarten.

The YMCA was and is a place apart: it hosted everybody, including Beitar's players and fans, who never lost their leanings to the right, since the early years until now. Prior to 1948, many of the Beitar players were members of secret armed groups like the Irgun. After the creation of the state of Israel, many fans supported the Herut party and, later, Likud. In fact, for dozens of years the hard core of Beitar supporters has belonged to the community of *mizrahim*, Israelis who came from Arab countries, the root of the Likud victory in the second half of the 1970s. What is most interesting, however, is the concept that the ultras of the Beitar Yerushalayim have of Jerusalem and their identity.

"Jerusalem is seen as a whole: the Jewish capital of a Jewish state. No Beitar fan would ever suggest it be divided," says James Montague, journalist and expert on Mediterranean soccer and, consequently, on the most popular and profound political traits and social dynamics. "The best way of looking at this is through the eyes of the people that have been attached to the club. Ehud Olmert, Ariel Sharon, Benjamin Netanyahu; they have all worked for the club or been keen fans," explains Montague. "The ownership of the club has changed hands to foreign buyers who see investing in Jerusalem as a religious and political duty."[42] This is the case with the last owner, Arcadi Gaydamak, the controversial Russian-born tycoon. It is no coincidence that his decision to acquire the club came at about the same time as his candidacy for city mayor.

The damage to the unwritten truce of Malha Mall by the Beitar Yerushalayim extremists, however, indicates something else unspoken: a contrasting identity that is alive and prolific. Us as opposed to them is one of the most classic and codified racist attitudes. We and they are always separated by a more or less visible barrier, depending on the case: a barrier that, in some cases, also hides the history of the conflict.

Behind the White Railings

"That one, that's the son of Begin. Be careful." The woman has untidy, almost disheveled hair. She is a heavy-set woman, with black hair of a mahogany hue, extremely dark and penetrating eyes, unkempt clothes, and a black coat. She enters what was once the cafeteria used by patients of Kfar Shaul Mental Health Center, the oldest and most important in Jerusalem. The oval arches, the vaults that form a semi-ellipse, the wide columns with old agricultural instruments propped against a stone projection, betray the age of the cafeteria that was once a house. Somebody else says that, perhaps, it used to be a public building, given that the column near one of the walls probably dates back to the Crusades. The woman with the dark eyes has a somewhat impudent gaze. Her comment, spoken almost deliberately in front of strangers, was addressed to the director of Kfar Shaul's emergency services, Gregory Katz, a psychiatrist and specialist in what is known as 'Jerusalem Syndrome,' a mental illness probably induced by proximity to religious sites that can lead to psychotic identification with biblical characters.

Katz, a Russian immigrant with a gentle expression, calmly takes no notice. The woman would seem to be one of the patients of Kfar Shaul, which offers a wide range of mental health services, from hospitalization to psychiatric visits to outpatient services. Yet that sentence, "That one is the son of Begin," cannot go unnoticed in a place such as Kfar Shaul Mental Health Center. It seems a bit like a practical joke of fate, or rather proof that history never fades.

Kfar Shaul was Deir Yassin. In 1948. Before 1948. The village of Deir Yassin symbolizes in Palestinian memory the horror of an intentional massacre, as attested by all historians—Israeli and Palestinian—who carried out research on the conflict. It was April 9, 1948, a few days before our Michel, the old inhabitant of Musrara, left his house to flee the war and take refuge in Beirut. The Stern Gang and the Irgun entered Deir Yassin, a village that, given its position, was a strategic target, since the road to Jaffa and Tel Aviv could be controlled from there. Highway No. 1, the great road that connects Jerusalem with Tel Aviv, still passes in the valley below. The stories are always the same. The Zionist paramilitary units entered the village, assembled the inhabitants, and were not content with killing them: they humiliated and tortured them without pity for the gender or age of those who confronted them. According to the most conservative estimate, more than a hundred were killed. The others, the survivors, were loaded on trucks and 'paraded' through the center of Jerusalem, before being left in Musrara.

The best-known representative of the Irgun is undoubtedly Menachem Begin, whose biography includes the massacre of Deir Yassin as one of the Irgun's leaders, in addition to the peace deal he signed with Egyptian President Anwar Sadat some thirty years later. It would seem that this historic mark is still imprinted on the memory of a woman in the alleys of the Palestinian village of Deir Yassin, which has become an Israeli mental health center, in a neighborhood named Kfar Shaul. Nowadays it is situated in West Jerusalem, a short distance from the highway to Tel Aviv, exactly in front of the hill on which the Holocaust Museum, the Yad Vashem, has been built. The madness of reality, unexpected, is even more surprising than fantasy.

Nevertheless, the patient's deliberate sentence, spoken on a sunny winter day, cannot be considered out of context. The madhouse of Jerusalem is the village of Deir Yassin, or vice versa. Its little houses, the grating that closes what was once a stable, the arched windows, the stairs marked by wrought-iron banisters, the traditional flat Arab roofs, the rough stones covering the external walls. And then there are the narrow alleyways, climbing the slope on which the village is spread. Deir Yassin's city setting is still very visible from the highway that goes around it, along which school after school has been built over the years. The old village lies on the other side of a fence, among the shouts of children and the silence of a small park, pine trees, soccer fields, a few cars passing by. Kfar Shaul Mental Health Center would seem a peaceful place at first sight. And Deir Yassin would have been a typical country village, rising to the top of a hill along a gentle but stony slope like the stony slopes that surround Jerusalem to the north. It is difficult to imagine something so terrible in such a pleasant and at the same time so anonymous a spot. But Jerusalem often hides within its normality the stratification of struggles, mourning, histories, memories, and the diverse identities of its protagonists. It is the same for Musrara, for Malcha, for the Old City, and for the two Jewish temples that became through history the Muslim Noble Sanctuary. It is the same, also, for Deir Yassin, now named Kfar Shaul.

The persistent past leaves traces in the folds of the present. The marks are visible. Simply crossing the main street in front of the mental health center, walking about two hundred meters, and leaning over the little stone wall—framed by a building on the right and a metal plaque that announces the construction of another residential center sponsored by the Jewish community of Venezuela—one sees a little wall that delimits a slope, with some trees, stones, and, most of all, trash thrown everywhere. By straining one's eyes, one or two Muslim graves can be seen. The stones are not cared for, many are broken, some of the graves are exposed. To the side there are trash bags, an aluminum saucepan, bottles, and cartons. This was the cemetery of Deir Yassin, and passersby know nothing about it because nothing is written on that little stone wall.

Shortly after the end of the war, the Palestinian village was not destroyed. It became, in fact, a welcome center for the new wave of immigrants, large crowds arriving from Europe. Jewish refugees from Nazi and fascist persecution, survivors of the Holocaust, the immigrants were divided among three different centers opened in Israel so that they would be able to begin a new life. One of these centers was put up in a place that had quite a different meaning for Palestinians. It meant persecution. There were even Jewish intellectuals of the caliber of Martin Buber who protested against erasing the memory of Deir Yassin with these new purposes. "The episode of Deir Yassin," wrote Buber, together with Akiva Ernst Simon, to the father of the Israeli nation David Ben Gurion, "is a black stain on the honor of the Jewish people. . . . It is better for the time being to leave the land of Deir Yassin uncultivated and the houses of Deir Yassin unoccupied, rather than to carry out an action whose symbolic importance vastly outweighs its practical benefit."[43] In other words, there was a request for the Palestinian village to be left empty and desolate, as "a *terrible and tragic symbol* . . . and a warning *sign* to our people that no practical or military necessity will ever justify such terrible murders."[44]

Buber and Simon's request to Ben Gurion went unheard. Deir Yassin was repopulated from the very beginning as a welcome center, and the whole area was given the name of what today is a densely populated area with a religious connotation—Givat Shaul. In the life of Israelis in Jerusalem, Givat Shaul has nothing to do with the old village, except for the anonymous little white gate, a passageway for cars, that leads to the mental health center. Apart from that barrier, the village of Deir Yassin seems surprisingly stuck in time, its urban and architectural integrity saved by the decision to open Jerusalem's mental hospital precisely among those alleys and little stone houses. Deir Yassin is today a mental health center in the most hidden place possible, veiled from public view, confined.

Amid those narrow streets, hidden from the eyes of 'normal' life, resided some survivors of the Holocaust, whose trauma from the death camps was deeply etched in their flesh and in their minds. The first of the Kfar Shaul patients died on January 10, 2011, and he was the first of a group who were survivors of the Shoah. At the time of writing, only two patients from this group are still living within the fence that protects the center from the harshness of daily life. It is the same fence that hides Deir Yassin from the gaze of those who survived the massacre of April 9, 1948, and their heirs.

Roland Barthes in Jerusalem

The classic reading of Jerusalem is as the archetype of the desired city, as the heart not only of world peace but especially of the pacification of souls. It is as if this place was the inspiration for Chloe, one of Italo Calvino's *Invisible Cities*. Chloe, "the most chaste of the cities."[45] The vision of Jerusalem as a pious place, however, clashes with the prosaicness, often the vulgarity of the daily displeasure of life. It clashes also with the real dimension of the city that is totally political. How then can it be read as "the most chaste of the cities"? Perhaps if we follow the imaginary thread traced by Calvino in the chastity of the city of Chloe, the reading would be different. Completely different.

> In Chloe, a great city, the people who move through the streets are all strangers. At each encounter, they imagine a thousand things about one another; meetings which could take place between them, conversations, surprises, caresses, bites. But no

one greets anyone; eyes lock for a second, then dart away, seeking other eyes, never stopping. . . . And thus, when some people happen to find themselves together, taking shelter from the rain under an arcade, or crowding beneath an awning of the bazaar, or stopping to listen to the band in the square, meetings, seductions, copulations, orgies are consummated among them without a word exchanged, without a finger touching anything, almost without an eye raised.[46]

"A voluptuous vibration constantly stirs Chloe, the most chaste of cities," concludes Calvino. "If men and women began to live their ephemeral dreams, every phantom would become a person with whom to begin a story of pursuits, pretenses, misunderstandings, clashes, oppressions, and the carousel of fantasies would stop."[47] If Calvino's vision were to come true, Chloe–Jerusalem would no longer be "the most chaste of cities" but rather "the best."

The reality is that Jerusalem is a mosaic composed of little tiles, like those that immortalize it in the frieze in Santa Maria in Trastevere. How then can we read Jerusalemite urban fabric? Perhaps to understand it we could use the tools of urban semiology, as Roland Barthes intuitively suggested when he described himself as an amateur in his observation of the city.[48] As a semiologist, he asked himself how it would be possible to investigate the urban fabric using tools different from sociology, history, and literature. It was in 1967, when he was thinking about urban semiology, that is, 'the science of signs' applied to town planning, and proved to coincide in a singular way with one of the cardinal dates in the contemporary history of Jerusalem.

If the city is a discourse, wrote Barthes, it must then be a language for all intents and purposes, composed of signifiers and meanings, of forms and significance. Why not then deconstruct it and understand what its signs mean? Why not go beyond shades, details, hints, even mystifications, and catalog instead the qualifying signs, the contents of city planning, the functions and styles of the city? Unquestionably it is fascinating advice, coming from one of the fathers of the 'science of signs,' because Barthes is willing to make order out of a city that at times is impossible to describe because it is so stratified, complex, and rooted in conflict. Perhaps semiology applied to urban complexity is precisely the only instrument to use, like a dictionary capable of translating Jerusalem. Translate it and then, for example, explain it, even to tourists, and especially to Christian tourists, who choose a destination like the Holy City often only by virtue of religious belief.

Religious tourists generally arrive in the city with heavy luggage: they have learned about Jerusalem through important and intangible readings digested in the course of their lives as more or less devout Christians. They seek out, sometimes with an insatiable, bulimic attitude, all the Stations of the Cross, step after step, in a rigid and exact sequence as determined by sacred readings, revelations, sorrows, miracles, and amazements.

The Via Dolorosa, the Holy Sepulchre, Golgotha, Gethsemane, the Last Supper, the Tomb of Mary, the place of Ascension . . . Jerusalem is almost reduced to a series of stops, without a broader, fuller view. The city is a list of evocative places that pilgrims believe are found in a celestial Jerusalem, reproduced on Earth, whittled down by the ugliness of daily reality. Most pilgrims repeat to those who live in the city that they were disillusioned by the Via Dolorosa because they had imagined it as being different. The fact is that the traces of the Way of the Cross must be uncovered, sometimes with difficulty, even in the markets in the Muslim quarter, among the shirts and souvenirs, among the street vendors and the butchers. Yet, while maintaining a discreet silence, pilgrims communicate by their expressions that they would prefer a Via Dolorosa cleared of daily life, sterilized, without the shops and businesses that invade the alleys of the Old City, for the merchants of today resemble the ancient traders in the temple.

This mundane Via Dolorosa is as similar to an evangelist's description as might be found in postmodern Jerusalem. It is a 'sign' of the solitude and passion of Christ in the daily dimension of the city: the same as, in the time of the historical Jesus, Christ himself being led along his Via Dolorosa among the market stalls, exposed to public mockery precisely in the places where the most people could participate in his humiliation. Even then, the small number of stations of the Way of the Cross indicated how few men and women among the mass of spectators came forward to offer comfort to a suffering man, or simply glanced up from their own daily affairs, in the market precisely.

For many tourists, including those who are religious, Jerusalem in its Old City—closed like a jeweled chest by the ancient walls—should by vocation be a museum that gathers its myths and displays its (spiritual) treasures amid a just light, a rarefied atmosphere, and fitting meditation. The sacred stones of Jerusalem should be as cared for and maintained as all reliquaries.

The sacred stones of Jerusalem, the stations, the temples dedicated to the various gods who are united in the City of Peace are, instead, merely signs, the *sema* of urban composition; signs that are understood, in all their power and immortality, only when combined with the people living nearby.

Staying only within the dimension of the Christian faith in Jerusalem, it is not possible to have an individual pilgrimage to the Holy Land without encountering the people who live around the sacred stones or seeing Christ in them, whatever faith they belong to, whether they are throngs of Palestinian workers at the checkpoint by Bethlehem, the wounded, the dead, or Israeli victims of a bus explosion set off by a Palestinian suicide bomber. Christ is everywhere, in Jerusalem, even for those without faith, or those, shall we say, without the necessary bare minimum of faith. It is enough, for example, not only to seek in the Via Dolorosa the classic stations, like that of Simon the Cyrene who helped Jesus carry the cross or that of Veronica who dried his blood and sweat, but also to look for other signs and imagine how people are living beyond the small iron gates glimpsed between the shops, how some of the real inhabitants live in Jerusalem.

3

A GAME OF *RISK*

A man was going down from Jerusalem to Jericho . . .
— The Gospel According to Luke,
The Parable of the Good Samaritan

Everything is just the same as it was thousands of years ago. Or at least, that is the illusion. The view is quite endless. Down there is the Dead Sea, the Jordan Rift Valley. There is also the desert that continues as far as the eye can see, until it reaches a far-off land that rises sharply. In fact, when the sky is clear and the horizon is not obscured by heat, the hills of Jerusalem can be glimpsed, as perhaps they were seen many centuries ago by Christian pilgrims undertaking the journey of a lifetime, on foot, in order to kiss the footprints of Christ. This yearned-for and promised land was also seen by Moses, according to what is written in the Book of Deuteronomy:

Then Moses went up from the plains of Moab to Mount Nebo, to the top of Pisgah, which is opposite Jericho, and the Lord showed him the whole land: Gilead as far as Dan, all Naphtali,

65

the land of Ephraim and Manasseh, all the land of Judah as far as
the Western Sea, the Negeb, and the Plain—that is, the valley of
Jericho, the city of palm trees—as far as Zoar. The Lord said to
him, "This is the land of which I swore to Abraham, to Isaac, and
to Jacob, saying, 'I will give it to your descendants'; I have let you
see it with your eyes, but you shall not cross over there." Then
Moses, the servant of the Lord, died there in the land of Moab,
at the Lord's command.[49]

Many of those who are still arriving at Mount Nebo today seem to
adhere to what Moses/Musa thought or hoped for: to see the Promised
Land, to look at Jerusalem from close up, to draw nearer to their own faith.
But it is unnecessary to have such a deep faith to love Mount Nebo. It is
easy to be enraptured by the solitude and the bareness of the place. Mount
Nebo is little more than eight hundred meters high. It is no more than a hill
by European standards. Instead it is a mountain, according to the orogra-
phy of the area, because below it lies the Dead Sea depression, which goes
as far as four hundred meters below sea level and puts everything in quite
a different paradigm. Nebo is a lonely mountain, on which it is easy to get
lost for a while and forget. It is enough to have eyes, to gaze at and imagine
the great valley without the time that has passed and still continues today.

There was a man in our strange and complicated contemporary times
who loved that mountain and embraced it wholeheartedly. He would go
there whenever he could, after he began to live in Jerusalem in the mid-
1960s. He arrived in the Old City prior to the Six-Day War and remained
continuously for the next forty-four years, until he died. He would take
a bus from Damascus Gate, carrying a big bundle of papers and books.
He would go down from Jerusalem to Jericho, as Luke the Evangelist
said, together with anyone else who had to go to Jordan via the Allenby
crossing at the Dead Sea. Palestinians from Jerusalem made up most of
the man's fellow passengers. There was nothing formally biblical about
that journey—it was, in fact, entirely part of the history and chronicle
of the Israeli–Palestinian conflict. He would go down from Jerusalem
to Jericho, pass through the eastern part of the city, cross the Separation
Wall and the checkpoint controlled by Israeli soldiers. He would pass

beside the Israeli settlement of Maaleh Adumim, and next to the poorest of the camps of metal shanties where families of the Jahalin's great Bedouin tribe were living, in front of Good Samaritan Inn.

The road is scarcely forty or so kilometers long in the middle of the desert and amid the bare hills. As time passed, it became a four-lane highway, fast and short. In fact, the road from Jerusalem to Jericho embodies another architectural and infrastructural wedge that obstructs the two-state solution envisaged by the Oslo Agreement. It splits not only the desert but also the West Bank. It divides Bethlehem from Ramallah, and Hebron in the south from Nablus in the north.

Jericho is at the end of the journey along the highway from Jerusalem, just before the place where John the Baptist is believed to have baptized Jesus. And then, in the middle of nowhere, materializes another checkpoint controlled by the Israeli authorities: the Allenby border crossing. The area should connect the Palestinian territories, that is, the West Bank with Jordan, as the only passage viable for those who hold a passport issued by the Palestinian National Authority based in Ramallah.

The man who used to go down, often, from Jerusalem to Jericho, always chose to go to Mount Nebo via the Allenby border crossing. He did not consider any of the alternatives, less exhausting than the first one: the flight from Tel Aviv to Amman and then a taxi to Mount Nebo, or a more comfortable transfer to Jordan via the Sheikh Hussein Bridge, far in the northern part of Israel. No. He would reach the Allenby crossing and wait for the arrival of the bus that goes—once more in the middle of nowhere—along the empty, silent road that connects the West Bank with Jordan. It is the road that crosses over the Jordan River.

Nowadays it is hard to relate the pivotal moments of Middle Eastern history to the present-day rivulet that once was the Jordan River. And yet the bridge is an ineluctable part of the history and daily life of Palestinians. It bears the name of the most famous British general in the region's contemporary history, Edmund Henry Hyman Allenby, made Viscount of Megiddo and of Felixstowe after the Palestinian campaign he led and the subsequent Ottoman defeat. Allenby was in some ways the last conqueror of Jerusalem, with his triumphant and yet respectful entry (deliberately on foot) to the Old City on December 11, 1917, through Jaffa Gate.

Yet the Allenby Bridge—better known as 'the Bridge'—is a landmark in the collective memory of Palestinians, more than in the Middle Eastern historical narrative. Portrayed in the pictures of the Nakba, the Bridge epitomizes the flight, the loss, and the misery. It is the bridge that witnessed the plight of Palestinian refugees in 1948 and in 1967, and it is the same one over which the Palestinians, as emigrants, return home from the Arab Emirates or the United States. It is the Bridge that Palestinians must cross if they wish to go on vacation, study in the United States, or seek medical treatment in Egypt. On the other side of the Bridge are the Jordanian authorities, who do not stamp passports, because this is not a border crossing but merely a transit station. It will become a border if and when there is a stable and lasting peace between the Israelis and the Palestinians. It will be a border crossing when the Palestinians are able to control the frontiers of the state of Palestine. Allenby's is only a crossing—controlled by Israeli military personnel—between the Occupied Territory of the West Bank and the sovereign state of Jordan.

After crossing the Allenby Bridge, travelers go across kilometers of asphalt in a barren landscape, and when they arrive on the Jordan side they are greeted by friends, relatives, and cheap taxis to take them, for a few dinars, to the large pleasant hotels along the Dead Sea, or to Amman. Or even to Mount Nebo, to the parish the man from Jerusalem led for years.

The man who used to come down from Jerusalem to Jericho never complained about the recurrent journey to the mountain from which it is said that Moses saw the Promised Land. On the contrary, when he was in Jerusalem he used to give advice on the Allenby Bridge's bureaucratic rituals to his friends, over a good cup of espresso made on an electric stove, in a tiny kitchenette, by a window in the Franciscan Monastery of the Flagellation along the Via Dolorosa. His studio was filled with bundles of papers, rolls of topographic maps, layers upon layers, and books in a particular disorder of which only he was the owner and custodian. "Try to get to Allenby by 10 a.m. so you won't have to wait long for the bus," said Fr. Michele Piccirillo, one of the most important archaeologists of the Middle East, a close friend of King Hussein of Jordan. He was Franciscan in flesh and heart, in his gentle madness and his love of the 'last.' And when I asked him why he did not use his position, his fame, and his experience to spare his energy and be treated as a VIP like journalists and international dignitaries when crossing the Allenby Bridge, his scornful reply was, "But no, I don't get annoyed! I read my students' dissertations and work hard."

Fr. Michele died too soon on October 28, 2008, in Italy. He had introduced into his personal history the parable of the Good Samaritan. As a Good Samaritan he helped the neighbor who had fallen in the dust in 1967, when, as a seminarian, he was one of the few who helped the inhabitants of the Mughrabi Quarter in the Old City of Jerusalem, built along the Western Wall. The Israeli authorities had bulldozed and destroyed the whole quarter in three days in July, a few weeks after the conquest of Jerusalem in the Six-Day War. "They did not let the Red Cross in. We as Franciscan seminarians helped the poor Palestinian families who lived in the Mughrabi Quarter," he told me with, as I read in his eyes, the same empathy as then. As Catholic believers repeat when they interpret the parable of the Good Samaritan, Fr. Michele received much from the gesture of helping his neighbor, as believers receive a sign from their god. He also received much from the places he lived, as Jerusalem and Mount Nebo profoundly changed his life. "From the mountain from which Moses directed his gaze of hope for the future, I too try to look ahead seeing so many young men ready to live in peace in a world that is fed up with war and hate," wrote Fr. Michele.[50] Now that his body rests, as he wished, beneath a great tree in front of the little convent of the Nebo parish, Fr. Michele is not far from Jerusalem. He gazes at it with the eyes of a pilgrim.

Your Neighbor

Even Good Samaritan Inn has changed over the years. Even in a place that became the archetype of immobility, in a place at the heart of the world and of unforgettable history, even the patch of desert involved in the parable narrated by Luke the Evangelist, has undergone the transformation of time. Today Good Samaritan Inn is a little museum built by the Israelis. It accommodates pilgrims who make their way from Galilee, along the Jordan valley and the Dead Sea, to their goal: Jerusalem.

The city is not yet in sight, as the highway continues to clamber over the desert hills. The village of Khan al-Ahmar opposite Good Samaritan Inn is barely visible. Some corrugated metal huts are hidden behind the hollow that forms a natural parking lot for old sedans and third-rate pickups down near the road. Khan al-Ahmar is only one of the little encampments around Jerusalem where the Bedouins of the great Jahalin tribe live in the depths of humiliation, after Israel expelled them from the Negev Desert in the 1950s. They are not allowed to build in the encampment sites because they are in the so-called Area C, as defined by the Oslo Accords. In brief, less than two-thirds of West Bank land has been classified as Area C and is under full and exclusive Israeli military and civil control. Israel prohibits Palestinian construction and development for the most part in Area C, arguing various rationales. In the case of the Jahalin encampment, the area is deemed sensitive from the viewpoint of Israel's security.

Khan al-Ahmar is a shanty camp where two hundred and fifty people have lived for decades. For years the Jahalin encampment has been the focus of a unique legal argument between the Bedouins and the Israeli authorities. An Italian nongovernmental organization, *Vento di Terra*, or Land Wind, had a revolutionary idea for how to bypass the unattainability of the Israeli building license for which the Jahalin yearned. *Vento di Terra* started with a building for public use. Its architects erected a school without foundations, made of tires and mud—they built a temporary structure exempted from the license requirement. Instead, the school met other less bureaucratic requirements. It allowed Jahalin children to avoid the long trip they had to make on foot to reach the school, from as far away as Jericho, some kilometers further along the highway. Over the years, that journey had become a nightmare, as many children had died in road accidents.

Three small one-story constructions made of old tires filled with mud, covered with a wooden roof, completely protected from the winter wind and the hot desert summer—this is the school of tires, built by the Bedouin. It is an example of sustainable architecture, far from the superabundance of concrete that has flooded Jerusalem both in the Old City and in the suburbs, which have gradually filled with buildings, settlements, streets, and walls. Although beautiful and perfectly blended with the chromatic view of the desert, the school of tires has not had an easy life since it was completed. The Jahalin community underwent an exhausting legal ordeal of demolition orders, petitions, and requests to move the school a few meters further from the highway. For years, the school of tires was saved only by the international press preventing its destruction.

From the Israeli point of view, there is an original sin in Khan al-Ahmar. The little school of tires is an accomplished fact, and it turns the camp into a less temporary shelter. Therefore, Khan al-Ahmar is more than before a wedge between the highway and the Israeli settlement—with, of course, its solid houses made of concrete—built a small distance from the Jahalin camp, just over the slope beyond. Ahead, in the direction of Jerusalem, there is the large settlement of Maaleh Adumim, sheltered on a hill, about forty thousand inhabitants strong, officially declared a municipality by the Israeli authorities in 1991.

Why has Khan al-Ahmar, a minute, almost forgotten Bedouin camp, become over the years something of a diplomatic issue? Why does a school of tires and mud cause scandal? Because by its very presence it reveals something that is happening now and will happen in the near future in and around Jerusalem. The small Bedouin camp, no longer so temporary thanks to the school of tires, breaks the geographic and political strategy of the settlements around Jerusalem. It prevents a connection between Maaleh Adumim and the Israeli settlements along the Jerusalem–Jericho route. A long corridor has been built over the years across a stretch of asphalt and a complex system of settlements, disconnecting the northcentral West Bank (Ramallah–Nablus) from the southern (Bethlehem–Hebron) and so dividing Palestine into cantons. Thus, the site of the parable of Your Neighbor, as told in the Gospel of Luke, becomes the symbol of a geography bowed down by the Israeli–Palestinian conflict, among confiscated land, settlements, and lawsuits.

Khan al-Ahmar's school of tires is just a detail in the complex tableau of the Jerusalem 'great game.' The tableau's core is at a short distance, a few kilometers away from the Bedouin encampment. It is called the E1 zone, at the center of the great international diplomacy, along the same highway from Jerusalem to Jericho, directly opposite Maaleh Adumim and the offshoots of East Jerusalem. The E1 zone lies at the back of the Palestinian quarters to the east of the Green Line, and it hosts already the incumbent gray building of the 'Judea and Samaria District Police' headquarters.

The story dates back to 1999, when the E1 master plan was approved. It envisaged thousands of residential units and ten hotels. At the end of 2012, the government, led by Benjamin Netanyahu, reiterated its will to implement the E1 plan, which will harm the West Bank as a whole. As B'Tselem, the Israeli Information Center for Human Rights in the Occupied Territories, stated, "Implementation of the E1 plan will have significant repercussions for the entire population of the West Bank. . . . Construction in E-1 will further reduce the already narrow corridor that connects the northern and southern West Bank and will impede the establishment of a Palestinian state with territorial contiguity." In addition, "construction in E-1 will enclose East Jerusalem from the east and link up with the Israeli neighborhoods built north of the Old City."[51] In brief, the E1 plan would close the pincers around East Jerusalem and compress the Palestinian population within an encircled area defined by the Wall of Separation, by Maaleh Adumim, and the checkpoint that limits entrance to Jerusalem.

From Good Samaritan Inn, from Khan al-Ahmar, in fact from the E1 zone, Jerusalem is still only an idea: a city that cannot yet be seen. Believers on tourist buses would approach the city with their souls full of questions and emotions. Yet, Khan al-Ahmar, Maaleh Adumim, the E1 zone are the heart of Jerusalem's destiny. They are physical symbols of the conflict, although unintelligible to the eyes of tourists or pilgrims, whose buses hastily pass along the route approaching the Holy City. They are even supposedly invisible to the eyes of the broad international community that reads Jerusalem through different interpretive lenses, whether religious or political.

In fathoming the real and contemporary city, the tourists' conventional guidebooks are almost useless. They are extremely detailed when it comes to each and every stone with the slightest tie to religion. But they do not grasp the real city. Perhaps other interpretative tools are necessary, in order to comprehend new urban signs. Official maps and plans are the proper instruments for understanding the contemporary political destiny of Jerusalem, because 1948 is still the core of the conflict. It was 1948, indeed, the time when Jerusalem became for a few months a bubble within the Israeli–Palestinian conflict, as an autonomous urban body to be detached from the new territorial composition of British Mandate Palestine.

A Separate 'Body'

Lines, limits, walls, borders, here and there, near or faraway. Everyone has his or her own compass in Jerusalem. Everyone knows how to calculate the exact position in which he or she is. There are few other places in the world where the cardinal points are so important—decisive in more than one sense. What a contrast to be born in the eastern part of the city, instead of the western side. What a difference to escape from west to east, or to build houses on the eastern or western side of the Green Line. What a gap to live in the north or the south, and to work in the opposite direction. The pocket compass in Jerusalem both describes and locates each individual's position and becomes the inevitable guiding light of his or her existence.

However, east and west and north and south do not follow, as is commonly understood, the path of rites, of customs, of lives that unroll according to the slow rhythms of a family or a society: birth, growth, work, marriage, children, old age, death. And then, again, relocations, journeys, courtesy visits, jaunts beyond, even funerals. They do not follow the usual swing of the commuters, trains, highways, home and office, school, swimming pool: anchorages in the daily rhythm of life. Instead, the cardinal points of Jerusalem, unique in their category, follow the broken lines of history, the prevarications of international political actors seated around elegant tables in intentionally ascetic meeting rooms. The Jerusalemite cardinal points follow, above all, the thick lines of the pencils used from time to time by diplomats, the military, politicians, leaders, the points of which dig deep into geographic maps, like knives into flesh.

Speaking in more prosaic terms, every gesture in Jerusalem bends to the lines traced by 'diplomatic pencils' in 1948–49, and then—over the years—to the diggers that have bulldozed the land within and beyond the city's limits. From 1948 on, Jerusalem has been enclosed by the limits chosen and determined, from time to time, by the newborn United Nations, by Israel and Jordan, and then, from 1967 on, only by Israel.

In 1947, the United Nations Special Committee on Palestine (UNSCOP) recommended what got its place in Middle Eastern history as the 'partition plan.' According to Resolution 181, adopted by the General Assembly on November 29, 1947, the three-times Holy City was to be enclosed in a sort of religious–geographic district that declared its uniqueness from the point of view of faith. In sum, the United Nations allowed Jerusalem's religious distinctiveness to prevail over the quasi-normality of its political and secular geography and its complex web of relations with the rest of Palestine, with the state of Israel in the making, with the broader post-Ottoman world.

The *corpus separatum* project, as it was called in the United Nations plans, envisaged a body, a separate organism that would become a sort of international city. The significance of Jerusalem, its value, its memory, its very own story, could not be held hostage by just one of its components. It could not be just Jewish, nor just Christian, nor just Muslim. It could not belong only to the Israelis, whose state in the land of Palestine had only been recognized recently, nor to the Palestinians, who had left such an ancient imprint on the flesh of Jerusalem. The UNSCOP recommendations in September 1947 are very clear on the matter. The religious "justification" for the establishment of the *corpus separatum* recites: "Jerusalem is a Holy City for three faiths. Their shrines are side by side; some are sacred to two faiths. Hundreds of millions of Christians, Moslems and Jews throughout the world want peace, and especially religious peace, to reign in Jerusalem; they want the sacred character of its Holy Places to be preserved and access to them guaranteed to pilgrims from abroad."[52] Subsequently, the political justification necessarily intertwines with the religious one: "Religious peace in Jerusalem is necessary for the maintenance of peace in the Arab and in the Jewish States. Disturbances in the Holy City would have far-reaching consequences, extending perhaps beyond the frontiers of Palestine."[53]

The famous partition plan of 1947, with which the United Nations tried to establish the state of Israel and an Arab state in historical

Palestine, foresaw a third institutional subject. The 'City of Jerusalem' had to become the third post-historical Palestine's mosaic tile. The United Nations justified the creation of a *corpus separatum* by noting the "many difficulties of effecting a satisfactory division of Palestine into a Jewish and an Arab State," read the recommendations of the UNSCOP to the General Assembly, in September 1947.[54] The city of Jerusalem, according to the partition plan, would "be established as a corpus separatum under a special international regime and shall be administered by the United Nations," and its territory would "include the present municipality of Jerusalem plus the surrounding villages and towns, the most eastern of which shall be Abu Dis; the most southern, Bethlehem; the most western, 'Ein Karim (including also the built-up area of Motsa); and the most northern Shu'fat."[55]

It did not happen. Jerusalem is not an autonomous entity by itself, separated and detached from Israel and Palestine. Neither is it a divided body in the mind of the city's each and every inhabitant. Not only for Israelis but also for Palestinians, Jerusalem is one, and just one: there is not a Palestinian east and an Israeli west, as if in the history of the city the communities' sense of belonging could have been defined by the connection to a well-defined cardinal point. During the first half of the twentieth century there was not a Palestinian urban development in the east vis-à-vis the expansion of Jewish presence in the west. On the contrary, both communities developed their own—bourgeois—presence in the west because that was the cardinal point of the sea, and therefore of trade. The real estate properties in West Jerusalem, in 1948, were 40 percent Palestinian, 26 percent Jewish, with the remainder (almost 34 percent) belonging to the public or, even more often, to Palestinian religious institutions. This is not a detail. It contradicts rather our own western perception according to which the Israeli and Palestinian communities in Jerusalem belong, each of them, to a precise quarter of the city's compass. This is not the case.

The extraordinary and unique history of Jerusalem per se demystifies the clichés of east–west identity. Both the communities feel their Jerusalemite identity as one. They belong to one city that has neither east nor west, except for the embroilments of a very recent period in contemporary history, which stretches only a few decades. For thousands of years belonging to Jerusalem meant to be part of a city, and not of a small part of it. In its uniqueness, Jerusalem is still today a 'body'—a *corpus*—and it is completely 'separated'—*separatum*—from all the rest. Essentially, Jerusalem embodies its distinctiveness, even if a good part of the world wishes to have a say regarding a 'body' that lives according to its own rules.

It happened in Berlin and in Belfast. It occurred in every divided and contested city. And it happened also in Jerusalem. The 1948 division of the city has been perceived by everyone, and not just by one part of the population, as soul-breaking. "Jerusalem leaves a feeling of sadness in my memory," writes for instance one of the La Salle Catholic order's priests, George, from his convent cell near New Gate. Br. George wrote to a confrere, Francis, a letter dated February 6, 1963, conserved in the archives of the Lasallian College des Frères in the Old City. "The city is surreal, as if the division were a sort of evil mechanism set deep in the night by a demon, as if it were an obscene joke. But it is no kind of a joke, and the cruelty is reproduced in the walls, the barriers, the barbed wire, the guns and the soldiers."[56]

The Power of Names

The streets of Jerusalem have changed names often, according to whoever holds power. Street names are not a neutral issue: they define identities, especially in places deemed crucial to the cultural makeup of peoples and faiths. It happened in Europe as well, for instance in Soviet satellite countries. Changing the street names after 1989, that is, after the fall of the Iron Curtain and the Berlin Wall, meant clearly the repossession of a preexisting identity. National identity had to be considered no longer spoilt by an ideological superimposition seen as completely foreign, alien, inappropriate. Changes were made hastily, so rapidly as to create quite a lot of problems of reorientation. Beginning in 1990, changing the names of streets in Budapest, Warsaw, Prague, and East Berlin became one of the more obvious and common ways of freeing the population from the past. In Budapest the pre-1945 street maps were dusted off, just like old license plates, to bring down the communist regime for a second time, and even wipe away the memory of it.

Similarly in Jerusalem the streets' names are hostage to the war of identities. It is inevitable in what must possibly be the most contested place on the planet. The very name of Jerusalem won through at the end of an extremely long historical path in which the name of the Holy City changed repeatedly, according to the 'ruler' at the time: Yerushalayim, or 'City of Peace,' the most accredited version according to Hebrew tradition, and the Arab and Muslim al-Quds, or 'The Holy.' Gerusalemme, Jerusalem, Jerusalén for European pilgrims. But also Aelia Capitolina, as baptized by Roman Emperor Adrian, who wanted to eradicate once and for all the Jewish Yerushalayim that had been brought to its knees by the destruction of its determining religious symbol, the Temple.

The Jerusalem street guide suffers the same fate. It changes according to whoever holds power. Metamorphoses accumulate, particularly in the contemporary epoch, when the very dimensions and composition of the city are changing. The clearest example of the connection between names and power came during the mandate. The British, who ruled Palestine from the First World War, revealed, through the new street guide, all the secrets of their collective imagination, not very different from the Europeans' rhetorical/religious depiction of Jerusalem. Sir Ronald Storrs himself, the first military governor and then civilian governor during the British Mandate, explained how and why the streets should be renamed. First of all, *how*. Street signs would be replaced with ceramic signs characterized by two dominant colors: blue like lapis or apple-green like chrysoprase. The street signs in Hebrew, Arabic, and English were meant to adorn Jerusalem 'like a bride.' The *why* is inherent in the choice of the new names: the names of the streets in the new city, outside the ancient walls, are primarily names of famous British soldiers and Crusader kings.

Admittedly, modifications to street names during the British Mandate were the result of a consultation among the different sectors of the local population. The British authorities brought together in a specific ad hoc committee representatives of the various religious communities, thereby confirming that they defined the inhabitants of Jerusalem according to their faith and not according to the notion of citizenship. From the beginning, the governor's influence was blatant in the choice of names. Even more evident is the weight of the British collective imagination, whose ancient bonds with Jerusalem were part and parcel of the national history. Sir Ronald Storrs chose the names of the streets from among those of Crusader kings and warlords, showing a lack of tact for a tragic and cruel part of Jerusalem's history. The list is long: Godfrey de Bouillon Street, Tancred Lane, Coeur de Lion Street, and Baldwin Street in Musrara, the 'memory lane' of our Michel. The (partial) equanimity of Mandate Palestine toward Jerusalem's inhabitants can be tracked down in a street dedicated to the hero of the Crusades revisited from the Arabs' perspective, Salah al-Din; in another street, which skirts the walls of Suleiman the Magnificent, dedicated to the Ottoman sultan who had them built in the sixteenth century; and in yet another, dedicated to the Maccabeans. But next to it there is a street named after General Allenby, the victor who entered Jerusalem as the conqueror of the Turks. There is also George V, the sovereign who ruled the United Kingdom during the First World War. The avenue dedicated to him in 1924 by Mandate representatives together with then-Mayor of Jerusalem Raghib al-Nashashibi was, and still is, one of the most important streets of the city—one of those that withstood the change of power in 1948 and in 1967.

However, the departure of the British from Palestine and from Jerusalem in 1948 took with it many of their traces, street signs included.

With the birth of the state of Israel, the affirmation of the newborn state's identity occurred also through the imposition of cultural bonds that had the task of strengthening it. It is a necessity that was not limited to the consolidation period, the early years or decades of Israel's existence, but one that continues to be evident today. An example can be found in the habit of spreading symbols of the nation everywhere, particularly the flag. During their Independence Day, it is still a custom for Israelis to hang flags from their balconies or to travel with little flags fixed to the roofs of their cars. Displaying the Israeli flag, they are not celebrating their football teams, as would obviously be the case in Italy. They are strengthening their sense of a national community.

It happened also with the street names after 1948, especially in Jerusalem where the preservation of memory and the building of a national identity have always taken more delicate paths than in the rest of the country. In other words, substituting one history with another signified for the young Israeli state the strengthening of its self-awareness. In the words of Maoz Azaryahu, geographer, professor at University of Haifa, and expert in urban landscapes and memory, "as the result of commemorative street naming, history becomes a concrete semiotic reality."[57]

Azaryahu explains that naming a street indicates power, not only because it requires the necessary administrative authority but also because it signifies the reconstruction both symbolically and materially of a place's history. The Israeli geographer goes on to say that the weight of the simple act of naming a street "becomes apparent when the political role of history, as both a version and interpretation of the past, is considered." Furthermore, "political regimes and elites utilize history to legitimate their dominance and augment their authority." On the other hand, "a sense of a shared past is crucial to the cultural viability and the social cohesiveness of ethnic communities and nation-states."[58]

The name Shivtei Israel Street (Street of the Tribes of Israel) was certainly closer to the Zionist ideal than the old name, Saint Paul Street, chosen by the British authorities for the politically important street that ended in the Musrara quarter, starting from the walls of Suleiman the Magnificent. The choice to rename one of the streets of the new city, St. Louis Street, to the more evocative King Solomon Street was certainly more accurate to the idea of building Israel's identity around its connection to the biblical interpretation of its history. However, in order to strengthen the implicit covenant between the Israeli Jewish community and the newborn Israeli state, the ostentation of the inseparable bond between the sacred and the institution is not enough. Israel needed to display its historical political path, that is, the connection between the Zionist state and the ancient institutional path interrupted by the destruction of the Second Temple by the Romans. Similarly, Israel considered it unavoidable to building rapidly a strong relationship between (the most recent) history and its mythical symbols. Even a sign posted at a crossroads could be instrumental to making evident "a change of regime."[59] It is not by chance, therefore, that the avenue along the walls of Suleiman the Magnificent, already dedicated to the Ottoman sultan, is now named in honor of the Israeli parachutists who fought in the Six-Day War.

In recent years, street signs in Jerusalem convey several messages to the inhabitants. The first is the substitution of memory through the act of renaming. The second message regards the use and abuse of languages. More and more often the very name of Jerusalem has been quite merely transliterated, instead of correctly translated. The Hebrew version, Yerushalayim, has been transliterated in Arabic, almost always erasing from street signs the name of the city in the age-old Arab tradition, al-Quds. The same political attitude is behind the decision to rename districts, erasing in this way their history. Musrara becomes Morasha even in the Arabic script at the quarter's entrance, and this modification—like many others—coincides with the strategic and detailed erasure of Jerusalem's history prior to 1948.

Beyond the Borders

Time has inverted the observation made by Israeli philosopher Avishai Margalit in 1991 that "Jerusalem has always had more history than geography."[60] In recent years the ratio has been reversed. Jerusalem has more geography than history, in the sense that the space occupied by the city is gradually growing, and exponentially in the latest phase. Jerusalem is no longer the city of past centuries—even though loaded with importance, no longer the small, provincial, neglected city of the early years of the Ottoman Empire. It is the capital of Israel, the internationally unrecognized capital of the state of Israel. At the same time, it is the state's most populous city, because, in the reckoning of the inhabitants of Tel Aviv, those who reside in the vast hinterland, from Rishon LeZion to Petah Tikva, from Holon to Netanya and Herzliya, are wittingly excluded. In other words, from 1967 to today, Jerusalem has never stopped growing, because the city's entire political destiny is caught up in its expansion. The borders, already modified and expanded immediately after 1967, have been gradually stretched like elastic, to the point of including areas (to the east and south) that are part of the occupied city, and symmetrically carving the northern zone where the Palestinian demographic increase was concentrated.

Everything began the day after the Six-Day War when Jerusalem became unified under the Israeli administration.

After 1967, Mayor Teddy Kollek immediately revealed his strategy: to shift the demographic balance in favor of Israel by constructing whole settlements (as yet not built) inside East Jerusalem. It is the famous 'finger strategy,' in which the fingers represent the Israeli settlements wedged between one Palestinian neighborhood and another, within occupied East Jerusalem. Kollek's objectives were above all two: to attract the Israeli population to Jerusalem with an active and constant housing policy, and to make another division of the city impossible through the presence of Israeli settlements to the east of the Green Line.

"The first and cardinal principle in the planning of Jerusalem is to ensure its unification," municipal planners claimed in a 1978 report called *Local Town Planning Scheme for Jerusalem.*

To date this principle has been translated into two modes of operation: one is to mend the gash that occurred in the urban fabric when the city was split in two in the War of Independence, and to fuse the detached systems; the second is to build the city in a manner that would prevent the possibility of its being repartitioned along the line that divides the two communities. . . . The principle of building the city as a mosaic devoid of polarizing elements has had a substantial effect in determining the location of the new Jewish neighborhoods.[61]

The goal is clear, according to the Israeli planners: "Every area of the city that is not settled by Jews is in danger of being detached from Israel and transferred to Arab control." Therefore, "the administrative decision regarding the area of the city's municipal jurisdiction must be translated into practice by building in all parts of that area, and, to begin with, in its remotest sections"[62] and then, consequently, approaching the center of the city. This is a strategy that has been carried out with precision and persistence, as can be seen by overlaying maps of Israeli urban expansion in Jerusalem over the decades. The presence of Israeli settlements in the eastern part of the city has gradually increased in a systematic manner. So much so that today it is impossible, from maps as well as actions, to think of a division of the city along the lines of ethnic belonging. Jerusalem is a mosaic. There no longer exists an only-Palestinians east, but there does exist an only-Israelis west.

Certainly, the *Local Town Planning Scheme for Jerusalem* was not only the representation of a municipal policy, nor simply the planners' translation of the mayor's strategy. Kollek's policy on Jerusalem was the spearhead of Israeli central government strategy from 1967, whether under Labor or, after 1977, in the hands of the emerging rightist party, Likud. The decisions of the Israeli municipality of Jerusalem were in fact connected to state policy through a corpus of laws on the city, on its real estate, on property, up to the Basic Law: Jerusalem, Capital of Israel. In order to strengthen the juridical basis of the city's status from the Israeli point of view, on July 30, 1980, the Knesset passed a law that made Jerusalem the capital of the state of Israel, "complete and united," and located in Jerusalem "the seat of the President of the State, the Knesset, the Government and the Supreme Court."

Formulating a town plan for Jerusalem means—therefore—to step into the peace process. The two-state solution envisioned by the Oslo Accords, which has Israel and Palestine beside each other along the 1967 border, with Jerusalem as capital of both states, is no longer feasible. The city has a different demographic balance than in 1967. In occupied East Jerusalem there are two hundred thousand Israelis living on so-called public land. Moreover, recently the Supreme Court applied even on occupied East Jerusalem the Absentee Property Law of 1950, which transfers Palestinian properties in West Jerusalem and inside the country to the state of Israel. Whoever the owners of the land had been, Arab Jerusalem now has a different look, and the Palestinian neighborhoods of Jerusalem seem ever smaller spots on the map, where people live without being able to count on their own future.

Israel's demographic data is considered important—decisive for some when it comes to the debate on the country's destiny. The same holds true for Jerusalem, and it explains the obsessive precision with which demographers and authorities count births, deaths, and residents in the city. One thing is irrefutable: numbers clearly indicate how much Jerusalem has changed. In 1967 about two hundred and sixty thousand people lived in Jerusalem. In little more than forty years its population more than tripled, exceeding its quota of eight hundred thousand, according to the Israeli statistics of 2013. Half a million are Israeli Jews and around three hundred thousand are Palestinians. The place of residence, however, cannot simply be superimposed on the numbers of the two communities. The half a million Israelis do not live only on the west side of the Green Line. On the contrary, the half a million people who live to the east of the armistice boundary of 1949 are only 60 percent Palestinian. Two hundred thousand Israelis in fact live in settlements considered to be Jerusalem's most populous neighborhoods by demographers, and they are to the east of the Green Line. All the settlements are considered colonies by the United Nations—settlements constructed by the occupying power, Israel, in Palestinian territory. Ramot, Pisgat Zeev, Gilo, Har Homa— Israeli settlements in East Jerusalem—are on par with the colonies built by Israelis over decades in the West Bank, close to Nablus, Ramallah, Bethlehem, and Hebron.

At a glance, the strategy pursued by Kollek has unquestionably been a success. Jerusalem is united, it is the seat of the main Israeli institutions, it is the capital of Israel, it is the country's most populous city. Moreover, it is the urban fabric in which—more than in any other place—the diverse tribes of Israel live and coexist. Secular, modern religious, and ultraorthodox communities, the many Russian immigrants, the new citizens who have just decided to move to Eretz Israel from every corner of the world, the pre-1948 Zionist Israelis. Certainly the *ratio* of the demographic balance between Israelis and Palestinians has not achieved the hoped-for and long-awaited results.

The multiplication of Israeli settlements in East Jerusalem has not been enough to increase the proportion of Israelis to Palestinians. Over more than forty years there has in fact been a constant diminishment—in terms of percentage—of Israeli residents and a simultaneous growth in the Palestinian population: from 74 percent Israeli in 1967 to 64 percent in 2010, while the number of Palestinians is always increasing even to the point of reaching 36 percent of the total population of Jerusalem, despite the ever more stringent limits to which the Arab community is exposed. Family reunification was reduced to a minimum after the Knesset passed extremely restrictive legislation. Weighing as heavily as a rock on Palestinian residents is the threat of being deprived of the Jerusalem identity card—blue ID revocations have increased exponentially in the

last fifteen years, with a record 4,672 residential documents annulled in
2008 alone. Added to the ever more restrictive legislation are the de facto
expulsions from Jerusalem of Palestinians living in neighborhoods divided
from the city in 2003 after the construction of the Separation Wall.

It is not so much the shift in the demographic balance of Jerusalem
that represents the real change in recent years. Rather, the political and
human panorama of Jerusalem has experienced its most obvious change
with the breakthrough onto the scene, to an important degree, of new
promoters of the Israeli strategy for the future of the city. Settlers belonging to the most radical fringe vehemently support their own specific
master plan, that is, a real estate policy profoundly different from the one
conceived by Kollek.

The mayor of Jerusalem had a meticulous strategy: It was necessary
to build Jewish settlements wherever possible in East Jerusalem, but
they had to be separate from the Palestinian ones in order to preserve
within the Jerusalem mosaic a manifest and clear separation between the
communities. Jewish quarters beside Palestinian neighborhoods, 'mono-
ethnic,' homogenous, without ever giving way to a sort of 'melting pot'
town in order to avoid friction and tension between the groups. In a way,
Kollek wanted to modify the demographic balance of the city without
detaching from the politics of separation followed by the British during
the thirty years of their mandate. The model was that of the Old City:
distinct neighborhoods, defined by their religious affiliation, side by
side but never mixed. Kollek's idea permeated the urban landscape, and
Jerusalem today is the city that the most famous mayor of the Holy City
worked for. In the last fifteen years, things have changed faster and faster
due to the increased presence of a different kind of Israeli citizen and
Jerusalem inhabitant: the radical settler. The strategy of the settler organizations in fact is extremely different and can be summarized in a single
sentence: "The land must be redeemed," give back the promised land,
Eretz Israel, to the Jews.

The call to "redeem the land" has translated into the violent entry
of colonies into Palestinian neighborhoods. On the stage of Jerusalem,
therefore, Israelis are playing two different roles. The Israeli municipality of Jerusalem and the national government continue to seize land and

plan settlements in the eastern side of the city. Meanwhile, the settlers fight a different battle, for houses. They are not houses to be planned and built. They are houses, often old houses, inhabited, inherited, lived in. Settler organizations are making their way inside Palestinian neighborhoods through the courts, legal documents, old property deeds. At Sheikh Jarrah, at Silwan, at Ras al-Amud, all strategic suburbs around the walls of Suleiman the Magnificent in the eastern part of Jerusalem, Israeli settlers have decided to break up the homogeneity of the Palestinian areas. In this way ethno-political identity overcomes the compromise, because it is absolute.

It is as if, during recent years, there could have been maps on the desks of town planners and settlers like military maps used by generals in battle. Directories of real estate properties became the troops used to fight trench warfare that is both long and imposing. The simple conquest of a trench, that is, a building, an apartment, or a piece of land, is crucial to the future conquest of the entire neighborhood, from one quarter to entire sectors of East Jerusalem. In this real version of the *Risk* board game, it is enough to look at, to observe visually the pennants of the new, small 'conquered' quarters to understand the strategy that anticipates the inclusion of Israeli buildings and settlements inside the most populous Arab quarters. From south to north, Jabal al-Mukaber, Silwan, Ras al-Amud, the Mount of Olives, Sheikh Jarrah, Beit Hanina, they are all neighborhoods that surround the Old City to the east like a crescent, and connect Jerusalem with the West Bank. For settlers, gaining access in these areas is strategically the first step in cutting Jerusalem off from the West Bank and driving the Palestinian population further away in the direction of Bethlehem and Ramallah.

The goal is the same, pursued through different and more violent means: to strengthen even further the Israeli side of the demographic balance. Despite all the consequences of the case, including the exponential increase of internal tensions in Palestinian neighborhoods, little by little settlers seize a house and set in motion the security forces around the building on which they have placed a big Israeli flag, surrounding it with barriers, barbed wire, and video cameras. From that moment, clashes, even physical, are the order of the day. The small intifadas of Palestinian neighborhoods mark the nights and days in an explosion of violence and the sound of hurled stones, dealt with harshly by the police and the army, always inclined, for example, to arrest the minors who are throwing stones, young boys scarcely eleven or twelve years old.

The increase in violence has not stopped, nor does it stop the settlers. They are much more ideological and radical than those living in the large settlements in the northern areas of the West Bank, near Nablus. Anyone who in 2009 took up residence in a little house in the East Jerusalem neighborhood of Sheikh Jarrah, a couple of steps from what was the 1948–67 seam line, near the American Colony, the most charming hotel in the city, is prepared for anything. Entire families have been forcibly evicted from Sheikh Jarrah's houses as part of a wider strategic plan on specific East Jerusalem neighborhoods. As explained by an official United Nations source, the Office for the Coordination of Humanitarian Affairs in the Palestinian Occupied Territory, "in a number of cases, property expropriated by the Israeli authorities through a complex system of legal, administrative and institutional mechanisms has been leased or transferred to settler organizations." Or, "settler organizations have made use of the Israeli legal system to lay claim to property allegedly owned by Jewish individuals or associations in the occupied territory prior to 1948." Israeli courts in a high percentage of cases have ruled in favor of such claims, while efforts by settler groups "have intensified in recent years and are often accompanied by attempts to forcibly evict Palestinian families and communities to make way for new settlements."[63]

The property documents often date back to the nineteenth century or the early years of the twentieth century, when there were no diplomatic pencils crossing through Jerusalem and the city had not been split in half. They state that the former proprietors of the houses were Jews. Whether true or forged, the documents risk taking the lid off the Pandora's box of Jerusalem real estate. If, in fact, the mechanism of claiming houses were to be triggered, Palestinians would be able—in front of international courts, for example—to regain possession of their properties to the west of the Green Line. Whole (now historical) neighborhoods were built by the Palestinian middle class, that is, by rich families that decided to leave the Old City, especially between the nineteenth and twentieth centuries, and open themselves up to modernity. These areas are extremely interesting from a real estate point of view, consisting of high-quality Arab houses, among the most valuable on the housing market. For the time being these houses cannot be claimed retroactively by their Palestinian owners, even if they are in possession of notarized or registered documents. By means of the Absentee Property Law of 1950, Palestinian houses, land, and properties were transferred into the possession of the Custodian of Absentee Property, meaning the possession of the state of Israel. It did not take long for them to be placed on the private market. This double standard is contested by human rights organizations, both Israeli and Palestinian, once again united for fear that it will open a chapter of unforeseen outcomes. For settler organizations to reclaim retroactively real estate to the east would also mean that the question of Palestinian real estate to the west would be raised. These were once upper-class properties that bear weighty names such as those of the Nusseibehs, the Dajanis, the Husseinis, and the Nashashibi—some of the most important names of the Palestinian nobility.

The settler associations, however, do not seem afraid or worried about the danger of opening a Pandora's box by their legal actions. For more than forty years they have increasingly enjoyed the Israeli state's support, that of the Knesset, the ministries, and the bureaucracy apparatus, at different levels and sizes. In more recent years they have expressed blatantly their own 'road map,' evoking in this way the term used by the international community for the path of the Israeli–Palestinian peace process. The road map in the settlers' version is simple: it is written by God in the Torah, and it is more powerful than the political one. This is the position of Daniel Louria, one of the leaders of Ateret Cohanim, and it is the same for the other associations that, with similar tools, seek to 'redeem' as many houses as possible in the Palestinian districts of Jerusalem.

More than thirty years old, Ateret Cohanim is involved in the restitution claims of old Jewish properties. They buy properties that they claim were formerly owned by Jews, and restructure apartments. In other words, they are a real estate agency that specializes in a very specific area: East Jerusalem, or rather the areas of Jerusalem where the majority of the Palestinian population is living. Daniel Louria, Ateret Cohanim, and a dozen similar organizations have a precise political goal. They want to bring Jewish life and customs back to areas of Jerusalem where the inhabitants nowadays are all Palestinian. "For the Jewish people, the heart of Jerusalem from the religious, historical and traditional point of view is the Temple Mount and the surrounding area: The Mount of Olives, the City of David, the springs of Gihon, the Temple Mount itself. All that area that has an Arab majority today has been the most important site for the Jewish world. And we are bringing back our roots."[64]

The 'redeemed' buildings in Palestinian neighborhoods are all structured on the same pattern: small fortresses standing apart, with obtrusive armed surveillance. It is easy to identify them, because Israeli flags stand out from the roofs, often enormous banners that are meant to convey to the world, especially to the inhabitants of the area, that the situation has changed. Nothing is as it used to be. Take for example Abu Tor, a neighborhood considered in many respects a mixed one. It lies between one of the attractions of the city outside the ancient walls, the King David Hotel, and the secular and gentrified residential district of the German Colony. Abu Tor has remained in some respects as it used to be in the 1967 period: Jews on one side, Palestinians on the other, and in between the memory of a border that, until the Six-Day War, separated Israel from Jordan. The physical boundary no longer exists. The one in social and daily life remains. Invisible. Ateret Cohanim's building is the exception: a small two-story house, a wall, an iron gate, a private armed guard inside a large guardhouse, a monitor, and a walkie-talkie. The security is paid for by the Israeli government, according to Louria. In other words, what they live in the settlers' buildings is an armored life. They think it will be their daily life until one day they reach their goal: the 'redemption' of all Eretz Israel.

The map of Louria and his Ateret Cohanim already shows many flags, not only at Abu Tor but even in the Muslim quarter of the Old City. Also the former general and prime minister Ariel Sharon took up residence there, walking distance from the Via Dolorosa. Ateret Cohanim's fortified houses are now in the entire ring of neighborhoods around the ancient walls. Louria's organization shares the same map as Elad, another association mostly concentrated in the Silwan area, just outside the walls of Suleiman the Magnificent, along al-Aqsa Mosque. Elad manages and supervises the so-called 'City of David,' an archaeological site, cultural center, and diamond point in a public archaeological park that the Israeli authorities are planning and that may drive Palestinian inhabitants out of Silwan.

"Here, Where Everything Began"

The girl has a frank expression, open, simple. Her brown eyes pierce into the eyes of others. A black scarf with some pretty woven threads of gold, tied in the Jewish orthodox fashion, covers her fine hair above her pale complexion. Hers is not a simple guide's job in the archaeological site the City of David, almost attached to the walls around the Old City and in the shadow of the silvery al-Aqsa Mosque. The girl with the black scarf considers her work as a guide at the site as her own true mission. She explains the origins of the place, and hers, to a group of tourists going down into the depths of Jerusalem. "Everything began here in this place," she says with a great deal of emphasis. The tour company's efficiency is blatantly more American than Middle Eastern, and it channels the tourist group among excavations, findings, and an exciting subterranean passage that reaches as far as Hezekiah's Tunnel, the ancient tunnel that carried water from the springs of Gihon to the pools of Shiloah.

It is all written in the Torah, for the girl with the black scarf. It is thus not accidental if the young guide follows her intimate handbook that is full of biblical quotations. The stages of the City of David tour bear in fact the imprint of a special kind of archaeology. What has been found must be connected to the Bible. In other words, it must confirm what is written in Holy Scripture. And it must confirm that King David's palace was exactly there and that it was the institutional heart of the kingdom of David and Solomon. Everything there began around the tenth century before Christ. This interpretation has attracted not only a growing number of tourists and pilgrims to the City of David but also tough, critical attacks not only from Palestinians but also from sectors of Israeli archaeology.

The vast majority of scholars in fact challenge the thesis that remains of the palace of King David have been found because it is considered weak from an interpretative point of view. The find confirms rather the later presence of a Jewish governing center, toward the seventh century before Christ. The accusation is harsh: political archaeology was taking place in the City of David,[65] particularly because of the organization that finances and supervises the site, Elad. It is one of the most radical settler groups, founded in 1986 by David Be'eri, former official of a special corps of the Israeli army. Be'eri was interested in—even in this case, and using the same terms as Louria—"redeeming land and returning Jewish awareness to the City of David."[66] Elad, which has at its head some of the leaders of the YESHA Council, a powerful organization that controls the settler movement, began to manage and influence the excavations in the zone of Wadi Hilweh, in Silwan, in 1994. And then, gradually but rapidly, it transformed the excavations in an attractive site for religious tourism.

The City of David, in brief, must demonstrate for Elad that King David was there, that the ruins of his palace are there, that this is the place "from which everything began." A legitimate idea, in a way, were it not joined to a selective historical narrative, that puts aside everything that happened after King David, and especially all that happened after the destruction of the Second Temple by Roman Emperor Titus and the beginning of the long exile, the Jewish diaspora. Roman, Byzantine, and Arab testimonies do not have the same relevance for this kind of political archaeology as the Jewish presence in Jerusalem. The accusation made by scholars and experts goes beyond the excavations at the City of David, and targets the utilization of archaeology by Israel. Archaeology is often used to build a national identity, selecting what is emphasized, conserved, and shown to the public. It has left in the shade hundreds of years of history that still can obviously be found in every street of the Old City, in the stones, in the houses, and in the mosques and churches.

Indeed, in the case of Elad and the City of David, doubts concerning the selected historical narrative are even more profound, so much so as to be expressed strongly by the president of the Council of the Israel Antiquities Authority, the public institution responsible for supervising all archaeological issues. "The Israeli Authority for antiquities is aware that Elad, an organization with a declared ideological agenda, presents the history of the City of David in a biased manner," said Professor Benjamin Ze'ev Kedar.[67]

Despite this accusation and the implicit downgrading of the organization's scientific qualifications, however, Elad continues to influence everything that happens in the City of David. Be'eri's association exercises strong pressures on the municipal and the national authorities, and pursues with the same success its own idea. From the elegant tourist center beneath the slopes near the Old City, close to the gate that leads to the Western Wall, the settler organization wants to go into the heart of the district of Silwan. The excavations will stop for nothing, not even in front of the fifty thousand Palestinians who live in the neighborhood, a decisively strategic area, given that the quarter is attached to the ancient wall that surrounds al-Aqsa Mosque and extends to the opposite slope.

A glance at the steep slope will not ever be forgotten: it is a sort of *favela* perched along the hill, houses upon houses, buildings grown on top of each other, some of the highest-density homes in Jerusalem. Silwan is one of those neighborhoods that grew exponentially, starting in 1948, with the arrival of families fleeing from villages like Deir Yassin or Malha, to the west of what would become the Green Line. Following 1948, families fleeing from the war and from attacks by Jewish paramilitary groups were driven to settle in an urban area that already, decades ago, suffered the miseries of conflict. In 1929 began the depopulation of the Yemenite village in Silwan, where Jews of Yemeni origin cohabited with Arabs from the end of the nineteenth century. The upheavals of 1929, followed by the Arab revolt of 1936, marked the end of the Yemenite Jewish presence in Silwan amid accusations of pogrom and expulsion.

It is tough, therefore, the history of Silwan, a village district in which the Arab presence does not date from 1948, but even, some families say, from the time of Salah al-Din. It became even tougher with the recent start of the difficult chapter of demolitions. It is a chapter written in the cold bureaucratic and legal language of demolition orders, of heavy fines for houses that do not have building permits. The legal battles are fought in the small municipal court at the head of the Musrara neighborhood, next to the municipal palace and our Michel's 'memory lane.' Israel's plan is to transform as much as possible of Silwan into an archaeological park, starting from Silwan's very center, al-Bustan, 'the garden' in Arabic, which is located precisely beneath the City of David excavations.

Municipal authorities sent just under a hundred demolition orders to the owners of houses in the area, and the excavators in some cases have already begun their work. The result is a situation on the brink of explosion, with constant scuffles and clashes between Israeli police and residents, stone-throwing, teargas, the little weekly Friday intifadas, arrests, closures, arrests of minors. And Silwan is now constantly presided over by the trucks of the border police.

But the extraordinary case of the City of David goes beyond its specifics. It goes beyond the archaeological value of past, current, and future excavations. It indicates above all the Israeli authorities' attitude since the Six-Day War concerning the thousands-year-long history of Jerusalem. The Israeli narrative on Jerusalem aims to make Jewish identity hegemonic by reassessing or actually considering as an accessory the presence of other protagonists in the city's history. And again the example of the City of David helps us understand: the accusation Palestinians and Israeli archaeologists are making is that the excavations are trying to confirm only an interpretive theory but, to achieve this, they have set everything else aside—the Roman, Byzantine, and Arab presence. In other words, in the chronology of the long history of Jerusalem, the politics practiced by Elad in the City of David and by archaeologists in the Old City suggest that they highlight the Jewish presence and constrain that of 'others' in a sort of karstic dimension, like a subterranean river.

In the words of Michael Dumper, one of the most authoritative scholars on twentieth-century Jerusalem, "the simple addition of all the years that Jerusalem was under Jewish control since the earliest archaeological evidence of settlement in 1800 BCE, reveals that Jerusalem was under some form of Jewish control for little more than 10 percent of that time."[68] He is referring to historical phases that include the first Israelite period of David and Solomon, the Hasmonean and Maccabean periods, and the period of semiautonomy under the Roman Empire. In Jerusalem, especially, beginning with the enforced unification of the city in 1967, the Israeli narrative has tried to join point A, the period of David up to the destruction of the Second Temple, with point B, the creation of the state of Israel. Strenuous support for a special link to Jerusalem's history that belongs only to the Jewish people gradually erodes the historical, cultural, and archaeological memory accumulated over the approximately eighteen hundred years between points A and B. The strategy effects a kind of tight compression, if not in some cases an actual erasure of Arab, Palestinian, and even Ottoman history and identity in Jerusalem, tracing a continuous line from point A to point B as if all that happened in between was perhaps an accident of history.

The brilliantly obvious example is the great square in front of the Western Wall, the goal of Jewish pilgrims and of tourists from all over the world. As time goes by, the plaza is becoming increasingly the icon of Israeli identity, the destination of students as well as of soldiers just enlisted in compulsory military service. It is an open space that did not exist before 1967, which was created with the bulldozing of an entire quarter, the Mughrabi, just a few days after the end of the Six-Day War. The architecture of the Mughrabi quarter was an important part of the history of the Old City. It embodied almost nine centuries, given that it was founded in 1193 by the son of Salah al-Din, al-Afdal.[69] It was destroyed in about three days, in part to avenge the humiliations to which Jews were subjected in previous decades when they wanted to pray at the Western Wall and were often forbidden by the authorities from stopping in front of the rocks that recalled the lost Temple.

The creation of the empty space in front of the Western Wall and the radical change in perspective that now completely opens up the view of the huge rocks under the Temple Mount clearly represent what has taken place in the Old City since the forced unification in 1967. Simone Ricca describes it as the erasure "of the complexity of history and embarrassing presence of other people's heritages from centre stage, while the large plaza in front of the Western Wall has given the State of Israel 'incontrovertible' proof of its historic right of the city." Ricca is an architect and an expert in the reconstruction of the Jewish quarter of the Old City, partially destroyed and neglected under Jordanian control between 1949 and 1967. In Ricca's opinion, it was also the cultural role of Moshe Safdie, the renowned Canadian–Israeli architect who planned the Western Wall area after 1967, to favor "the intellectual removal of the Palestinian presence from the city (especially their claims of it) within international public opinion."[70]

One identity, Jewish in this case, is established at the expense of another, as has often occurred in world history, not only in Jerusalem. Whoever assumes political control of a place tries to erase the predecessors' identity in order to substitute it. Jews themselves experienced this to their disadvantage, when the Romans asserted their presence and power, and not just by destroying the Second Temple. The Romans actually went further, changing the name of Jerusalem to Aelia Capitolina and moving the city center so that it was no longer in a large and sacred space like the Temple Mount. In what remains until the present the Romans' mark on the city, they decided to locate Jerusalem's center around a column with a statue of Emperor Hadrian.

As a matter of fact, Hani Nour Eldin explains, the column, or the memory of a column, is the true heart of life in Arab Jerusalem. Nour Eldin is a Palestinian archaeologist at al-Quds University (the Arab university that now lies beyond the Separation Wall), himself a resident of the Old City and a descendant of an important old family. Even today, in the daily life of Palestinians in Jerusalem, "the meeting place is not the market, the forum, the open space. They meet at the Gate. That was where they used to meet, and still do." 'The Gate' is Damascus Gate, where the market, the exchange, the life of the Arab city are concentrated. Damascus Gate in Arabic is called, and not by chance, Bab al-Amoud, that is, 'gate of the column.' It is an ancient memory. It is the memory of the column on which the statue of Emperor Hadrian was placed. It is also the memory of a person who tried to revolutionize from above the urban fabric of Jerusalem in order to bring an end, in his own way, to the history of Judaism after the destruction of the Second Temple by his predecessor Titus. So Hadrian decided to give birth to Aelia Capitolina, to rewrite history in the stone with stones, to create another Jerusalem. The column with the statue of Hadrian in what is now the heart of Arab Jerusalem, Damascus Gate, is also the departure point for a long stretch of history, the true heart of the Old City: the Cardo, the axis that runs through the network of streets of ancient Jerusalem from north to south.

Today's Cardo is nothing more than ancient traces that can be detected in the urban fabric of the Old City. Even the street network is no longer comprised of the typical embroidery of intercommunal life and commerce. Until the advent of the British Mandate, Jerusalem was far more mixed in confessional terms than we could imagine. The British broke up the subtle and constant osmosis between the communities along invisible borders and seamlines, and subdivided the built-up areas inside the Old City into four administratively separate quarters. They eventually became fairly homogeneous sectors according to the ethno-religious affiliations of Muslim, Christian, Armenian, and Jewish communities.

Confined to old administrative border lines and new security-related limitations, the four quarters no longer share any common place. No streets function as they used to, as an axis through the Old City. The market inside the Damascus Gate is not the same. Not a single shared and public square can be found.

If the square is the epitome *par excellence* of a public space shared by all communities, of intermingling and the free circulation of people and relations, then Jerusalem lacks public spaces. It is no longer a city in the way cardinal Carlo Maria Martini described Celestial Jerusalem, a "city, a place where men live in harmony, in a weave of complex and constructive relationships."

Jerusalem is no longer a city. It is an urban body where the ongoing conflict has changed the parameters of coexistence, moving from open and shared social spaces to closed social spaces where access is limited according to ethno-religious affiliation. The limitedness and exclusivity of social spaces are best defined by the two most renowned squares, in fact the only two large squares in the Old City. The Noble Sanctuary and, just beneath, the plaza that leads to the Western Wall: one beside the other. They are endowed with an absolute religious connotation, or a deep political/religious meaning.

The Noble Sanctuary and the Western Wall Plaza are vast but not inclusive. They epitomize separation and exclusiveness in Jerusalem as a contested city. For Jews, the Noble Sanctuary is the heart of Judaism and faith. For Muslim Palestinians, the Western Wall is a denied place of faith, the Buraq Wall. It represents the erasure of Palestinian Jerusalemite history through the Israeli authorities' destruction of the ancient Mughrabi quarter in July 1967, just after the Six Day War. The squares are both exclusive places, almost forbidden to members of the other community.

Conflicting realities face one another much as they did in Berlin before 1989, which was another divided city. The eastern and the western sectors faced each other along the Berlin Wall, demonstrating to the 'other' its own perceived superiority through the magnificence of its public buildings, from the Staatsbibliothek and the Philarmonie in the western side to the Alexanderplatz on the eastern.

Just outside the gates that lead into the enormous Noble Sanctuary, the sounds of the Old City become distant noise, "faint in the late afternoon," as Pier Paolo Pasolini might have described it. Closed at two ends by the gigantic Dome of the Rock and by the delicate lines of al-Aqsa Mosque, the square is heartwarming for its breadth, so distant and different from the Old City's intricate network of alleys. Such also is the welcoming shade of its olive trees and ancient stones polished by time. It is a flat area where one can finally find breathing space after so much conflict. From the Noble Sanctuary, one's gaze can finally free itself and reach beyond the sight of the walls, , toward the slope of the Mount of Olives, and toward Mount Nebo.

Opposite the Noble Sanctuary and a little lower, the plaza of the Western Wall does not have the same visual sense of opening. It stretches in length toward Sha'ar Ha'ashpot, the Dung Gate, one of the entrances through the walls of Suleiman the Magnificent. The space has been planned and organized to situate the Western Wall in the center, making it the focus not only of prayers and devotion but also of one's gaze. The plaza replies to the silence that fills the Noble Sanctuary with a bustle of men and women, pilgrims, tourists, the faithful—the mass of people who fill the space as they admire the Western Wall.

The squares exist one in front of the other. The confrontation of the two squares *ad escludendum* is the architectural and spatial expression of their respective communities in an overcrowded urban reality. The Old City is predominantly narrow, comprised of little streets, alleys, and houses. As large and empty spaces, the squares are, therefore, a clear demonstration of power: open spaces that can contain the extensive and populous community of the faithful, in addition to the symbols of the faith itself.

The Hunger for Houses in the Shade of the Holy Sepulchre

The main entrance to the house is scarcely noticed by the crowds of pilgrims as they enter through the little alleys of the Old City of Jerusalem. It is just past Damascus Gate, five minutes' walk from the plaza of the Western Wall, and some ten meters before the fifth Station of the Cross, where the Via Dolorosa climbs toward the Christian quarter, hidden among clothing stores, dried fruit, and souvenirs. It is a narrow main entrance, as narrow as the awkward and steep steps that climb up to the tiny apartment of Amti Miladeh Zahran. A cuckoo clock just beside the entrance, a bedroom, a room into which three little divans are squeezed along the walls, with a low table in the center, and a very low ceiling above. "We built it ourselves," Amti Miladeh, a Christian Palestinian, tells us as she lights her umpteenth cigarette. "Upstairs, right above this ceiling there is another mezzanine. What looks like a frame it's none other than the base of the built-in bed where my son and his wife sleep." Thirty square meters, including the mezzanine. Amti Miladeh's little home is barely suitable for a couple with a small baby. Sixteen people have been living there for six years: Amti Miladeh, her husband, her son, his wife, their children, and so on.

It is a tale of difficult daily life, without physical space and without privacy, but it does not dampen the spirits of one of Amti Miladeh's grandchildren. It is lunchtime, and the young girl has just got out of Schmidt's College, one of the best girls' schools in Jerusalem, just outside Damascus Gate. She regrets the "old days," a childhood spent playing with her little cousins in that extremely tight space. Now they are living in Beit Safafa, a neighborhood to the south of the city, some hundred meters from the big Israeli settlement of Har Homa and from the concrete wall that separates Jerusalem from Bethlehem, dividing also the Palestinian Christian community. Beit Safafa is a quarter on the border, where many Palestinians, Christians and Muslims, have succeeded in finding a house to rent, but the rent is as much as 800 euros—impossible to afford for a family with an average income. However, there is no chance of finding a house in the Old City. It is full to overflowing, like Amti Miladeh's house.

Yet Amti Miladeh's small apartment means much more than a roof over their heads. It means that they are able to live inside Jerusalem's newly imposed borders. It is the same for the little house nearby, owned by the Franciscan Custody of the Holy Land, where Francis Faltas's family lives amid piles of furniture. "If we are here, it is because we moved back from Azzariyah, to keep our Jerusalem identity card," explained Vicky Faltas, a woman with a look of great sadness and no more hope, as she cooked for her family in a kitchen no larger than a pantry, crowded with plastic bags. Her tired eyes betrayed a wish to return to a dignity that she is rapidly losing.

To live in the city, to have a residence permit, means having the blue document, the blue ID. It is necessary to obtain it, to be able, in short, to reside within the boundaries of the municipality of Jerusalem as established by the Israeli authorities. But the boundaries have shifted from 1967 to today. Since Israel started to build the Separation Wall in 2002, the situation has gradually worsened, especially for those Palestinians—many of them Christian—who put money aside and bought a house in the residential neighborhoods toward Ramallah or in Bethlehem. Suddenly, they found themselves 'on the other side.' On the other side of a Separation Wall that diplomatic documents in 2012 described as at least 168 kilometers long within the area of Jerusalem alone, where only 3 percent of its length follows the Green Line.[71] Palestinians found themselves, overnight, in a territory where their identity card had changed color, from the blue of Jerusalem to the green of the West Bank. Azzariyah, a neighborhood that overlooks the Jordan valley and Jericho, the site of the Tomb of Lazarus, is situated on the other side of the Wall, yet it is at most two kilometers as the crow flies from the other walls, the ancient walls that enclose the Old City. And it is there—between the walls that seem more like the tall fence of a prison—that the Faltas family has returned, leaving behind a much more dignified house to resettle four adults in one room and an attic.

Many have made this journey back to square one. They have returned to the Old City and closed themselves into small houses, crowded and often unhealthy. And this is the reason why the overcrowding in the Old City is not sustainable, as it is becoming in border districts—so to speak—on par with Beit Safafa. These districts have become the basin in which those who want to maintain their status as Palestinian residents of Jerusalem have poured. The blue ID confers a very different status from the ID of a Palestinian in the West Bank, and is a thousand times better than that of a Palestinian in Gaza. This is the reason two hundred families have relocated in recent years from Bethlehem to Beit Safafa, leaving a house on the other side of the Wall and subjecting themselves to the high rents of Jerusalem's eastern areas. The Wall and the new city boundaries, in fact, have reduced the area in which families can find a house to rent, whereas licenses to enlarge apartments and construct additions to already existing buildings are issued only reluctantly to Arabs, as human rights organizations, both Israeli and Palestinian, have noted in many reports. For younger people, not finding a house means not getting married in a society where marriage, children, and families play a fundamental role in life's plan.

Those who experience the repercussions of Palestinian families' search for housing in East Jerusalem are Muslim and Christian religious institutions, which still have hold of a considerable amount of real estate in the city. First, the *waqf* as the authority of the Muslim religious endowment tries to meet the needs of its community. And then there are the Christian religious entities, from Greek Orthodox to Lutheran and even Franciscan. The Franciscan Custody of the Holy Land, caretaker of Catholic sites, has in recent years received a good seven hundred requests for apartments. The Franciscans have houses both in the Old City and in the Jerusalemite residential areas toward Ramallah or Jericho. For a Palestinian Christian family, getting one of those houses, for much lower rent than on the market, means hitting the jackpot.

The religious institutions' real estate holdings are part and parcel of the complex game of Jerusalemite *Risk*, in which every community tries to raise its flag on a piece of land. Even housing is transformed into a sophisticated and difficult political battle. And the battle over houses is decisive for the future of the city, especially in the eastern districts.

While the Franciscans open their houses to Palestinian Christians, in Beit Faji, where the Catholic tradition places the entry of Jesus Christ into Jerusalem, on the Mount of Olives, another flag has been raised. In a completely Arab quarter, an enormous Israeli flag hangs over a building acquired, through a mediator, by a radical settler association. There is also a compound of Israeli settlers in the heart of Ras al-Amud, a stage for ever more frequent clashes and protests.

It is as if all the parties involved have become aware that, now, the battle for Jerusalem might be fought in a small amount of time. The importance now much more than before, however, is to raise one's banner, to declare possession and sovereignty. What counts, here, is to build and acquire houses. Because architecture, like everything else in Jerusalem, is never neutral, so much so that houses become enemies of the city and its inhabitants. As is said of another 'cruel city,' Palermo, by one of its most impassioned poets, journalist Salvo Licata, "In the light of day / the people hide / In the company of its shade / Because they fear the neighbor as much as themselves / people turned pale from domestic enclosure / people ruined by houses."[72]

All this is known, and has been for a long time. It is not simply one observer's impression. We have it in black and white. It has been written about and denounced by United Nations agencies working in Jerusalem, which publish studies and articles on civil, political, and cultural rights in the city's various neighborhoods. Consul generals of European Union countries have documented and denounced it in the reports on Jerusalem they publish annually and send to Brussels, so that it can be taken into consideration in the European Union's political stance toward the Middle East. Piles of paper, packets, maps, and denunciations that remain dead letter or, after exhausting negotiations to soften the terms, are condensed into so few lines as to be lost in the sea of European foreign policy documents.

Harsh and precise words are used constantly by European consulates' heads of mission to describe the situation in Jerusalem. The 2012 report mentioned above confirmed, for example, that "if the implementation of the current Israeli policy regarding the city continues, particularly settlement activity, the prospect of Jerusalem as a future capital of two states—Israel and Palestine—becomes practically unworkable." Why? Because, according to the report, Israel "is actively perpetuating its illegal annexation of East Jerusalem by systematically undermining the Palestinian presence through restrictive zoning and planning, demolitions and evictions, discriminatory access to religious sites, an inequitable education policy, difficult access to healthcare, the inadequate provision of resources, the continued closure of Palestinian institutions, and the restrictive residency permit system." As if this were not enough, "the archaeological activity around the Haram al Sharif/Temple Mount exclusively stressing the historical connection of the Jewish people and strengthening Israeli control of the area, undermines the universal character of the city."[73]

Business as usual. The European Union Heads of Mission report on Jerusalem reiterates each and every year almost the same worrying picture of the city. Yet things started to change profoundly in 2014, after the most worrying cycle of violence in Jerusalem since the end of the Second Intifada. "Over and above the all too familiar negative trends," stated the 2014 report, the year "has been distinguished by a number of specific and often violent developments which are rapidly threatening the viability of the two-state solution, and which are also creating extremely high levels of friction within the city itself." The report noted, "If root causes of the recent violence are not addressed, the likely outcome is a further escalation and the extreme polarization."[74] And so it happened. The cycle of violence broke out in full force in 2015: Cassandra reloaded.

Homo Jerosolimitanus in the Making?

Many children are born in Jerusalem. More are born compared with the whole of Israel's Jewish population than in the rest of the country. Jerusalem, although considered (and perhaps despite being) the bulwark of tradition, is a young city. Half the population in 2010 was under the age of twenty-four. And, to be even more specific, half of the Israeli population was under twenty-six and half the Palestinian population was under twenty. A city of young people, and a city of children, as often happens in the Middle East. It is yet another of the profound differences that distances Jerusalem (and the Middle East) from Europe.

At first sight it is difficult to think of Jerusalem as a city full of children. In the western imagination the city of the three monotheistic faiths is seen and perceived as old, advanced in years. If anything, celibate and single, as if its population were made up of nuns, priests, men and women devoted only to a spiritual relationship with God. Instead, take a close look, children are everywhere. They go to school in droves, they play in the little parks in the orthodox quarters, and they invade the streets en masse on Shabbat, the Jewish Sabbath, at Mea Shearim and in the neighborhoods where the ultra-orthodox are the majority. They are just as much a visible (and audible) presence in Palestinian quarters. They, although not their parents, are allowed to play in the Noble Sanctuary, because everything is permitted to the innocence of children.

They feel the conflict, for certain, even they. They are perhaps the hostages of their parents, especially boys, and therefore they are the ones that, from one or the other side of the barricade, will pay more with their blood and lives. They are young children, girls and boys, who breathe the air of Jerusalem, which is different from the air that is breathed in other cities. They are girls and boys who see the different uniforms on the bodies not only of grown-ups but also of their peers. They begin right away to learn who belongs to their own tribe (ethnic, religious, political) and who, on the other hand, is to be kept at a distance. They look attentively at who is opposite, they know how to move about an urban setting where there are quarters that through different colors mark their otherness. They know the streets that are allowed and the streets that it is safer not to pass through.

The children of Jerusalem, whether Israeli or Palestinian, grow up faster than their contemporaries in Europe. Above all, they grow up as individuals, they mix little, they know practically nothing of each other. And yet, all together—willing or unwilling—they grow up. And they absorb from the city just enough to make them, Israelis and Palestinians, inhabitants of Jerusalem, with their own characteristics, different from those of contemporaries in Tel Aviv or Jenin.

Is there a *homo jerosolimitanus* in embryo? Indeed. But this does not mean that the new species of Jerusalemite knows that they have characteristics in common: belonging to a special city, different from all others; their minds trained to observe men and objects attentively and carefully; a rushed exit from infancy; a certain Spartan awareness of daily life and of objects. Certainly this is not enough to hope that new generations will be wiser and will help achieve a durable peace between Israelis and Palestinians. Above all because there emerges, clearly, the fact that these generations of Jerusalemites grow up far from each other. Far more distant than in the years of the First Intifada, for instance.

Interaction between the communities is extremely rare. It involves some places, and only some sectors of the urban population. Certainly it does not affect, for example, the ultra-orthodox—a very varied sector at the core, a galaxy full of denominations, specificity, rites, and customs, squeezed under one single umbrella, orthodoxy carried to its most literal consequences. The ultra-orthodox community represents almost 30 percent of the Israeli population of Jerusalem. Together with those who remain observant and observing traditionalist, they constitute a little less than two-thirds of Israeli inhabitants, a true and proper political–religious lobby that has a profound influence on the decisions taken on or about Jerusalem. These sectors succeeded in 2003 in electing a mayor, Uri Lupolianski. They were very persuasive and successful in arguing that some areas of the city should be off-limits to cars out of respect for a more rigorous interpretation of the Shabbat day of rest. They erected high obstacles to livelier tourism activities, trying to prevent, for example, a new parking lot near Jaffa Gate from being open on Saturdays.

The pressure the ultra-orthodox community exerts affects not only political decisions, but also, if not above all, the dimensions of separateness, the impermeability between the different worlds that inhabit the streets of Jerusalem. Discomfort is felt by Israeli secular groups in Jerusalem who abandon the city for a more comfortable environment—and a secular one—far from the heavily populated quarters where the ultra-orthodox presence has increased exponentially. This is awkward, and the resulting continual migration from one quarter to another reveals clearly the lack of Israeli homogeneity in Jerusalem.

There is continual clamor in a city that in itself is an icon of the Israeli–Palestinian conflict. Its clamor becomes noticeable when Jerusalem must deal with the rhythms of its tribes. When Shabbat approaches and the ultra-orthodox swarm toward Damascus Gate from Mea Shearim, the streets fill with holiday clothes, with whole families united, happy, moving together toward the Western Wall, proud of their faith, which they affirm even when in the streets. Or when the annual Jewish rites intrude on the very daily life of all inhabitants. This is a world that considers itself apart, and wants to remain apart, and at the same time—in obvious contradiction with its proverbial discretion and its refusal of contamination—is visible, increasingly more visible. At times it imposes its *modus vivendi* on other sectors of Israeli society that instead lay claim to space, and above all to time.

It is not simply a question of different rites, of a different conception of faith. From the demographic point of view, the rapid growth of the ultra-orthodox community in Jerusalem signifies a chromatic change that goes beyond the strictly homogeneous ultra-orthodox neighborhoods. A shift in the modest colors, traditions, women's dresses, and the black of men's clothes: the profound chromatic change is everywhere, on the sidewalks of commercial streets, in the cafes, in the parks, and most of all on the washing lines on balconies. The modest shop windows of the clothing stores frequented by ultra-orthodox families are in black and white, while the rows of shoes are all equal and all black.

But above all it is the cultural transformation of Jerusalem that marks the present, and perhaps the future, of the city, not only because the more religiously observant community influences the political balance of the city but also because it makes communication among the different demographic groups more difficult. If it is difficult for secular Israelis to interact with closed orthodox communities, it is even more difficult for Palestinians in Jerusalem. It is enough to turn one's attention to Damascus Gate during Shabbat to observe how ultra-orthodox families follow the same path, every week, walking on the same stones, without even a glance at the little stores before and after the ancient walls, at the children, the shopkeepers, the shoppers. It is as if they are on a bus, without any contact with the outside.

Until violence broke out in 2014 and 2015, Israelis and Palestinians ignored each other, except sometimes when the friction rose to a certain limit. A push, a spit, insults, and then they would all return to their ranks, ignoring each other, as if each one, within his or her own box, were transparent, impermeable to colors and to sounds, to any kind of cultural interaction. It all changed when violence broke out in the Old City, trespassing those accepted limits. It all changed when a special civil war broke out in Jerusalem.

4

(RE)BRANDING JERUSALEM

A stone's throw from Jerusalem
I walked a lonely mile in the moonlight
— Sting, "Mad about You"

The Tie and the Dome

It is hard to imagine what sort of man would wear it: a clumsy vaca-
tioner, or rather a somewhat irreverent hipster? He certainly could be
a man of devotion. But devotion to what god? Would he be a Muslim
or Jewish believer? The problem is that the tie for sale on a website of
touristy tchotchkes with a geographic theme is distinctive. It is kitsch,
like all tchotchkes. No doubt it is evocative, but ambiguous at the same
time. There are images of the Dome of the Rock stamped on the tie from
top to bottom, repetitive and excessive. Replicas *ad infinitum* that in their
repetitiveness dismiss the unique value of the monument.

So what? There should be no ambiguity in such an image. The Dome
of the Rock is a mosque. Together with al-Aqsa Mosque it represents the
third holiest place in Islam, after Mecca and Medina. For Muslims it is a
unique place because of its revelation: the Prophet Muhammad arrived

there by riding an unusual mythological creature, a winged horse with a human head, Buraq. The first verses of Sura 17 of the Holy Quran, al-Isra', say: "Glory be to He Who carried His servant by night, from the Holy *[haram]* Mosque to the Furthest *[aqsa]* Mosque, the precincts of which We have blessed. So that We might show him some of Our signs."

Muhammad therefore arrived in the city of the "furthest mosque," Jerusalem, the Arab al-Quds. On the rock near the "furthest mosque" he left his imprint, and then Buraq carried him up to the sky to see paradise on the night of the 27th of the month of Rajab, the seventh lunar month in the Islamic calendar. It is the miraculous night journey and ascension into heaven—*al-Isra' wa-l-mi'raj*—that Muhammad experienced. After that, the winged horse carried him to his point of departure, Mecca. It is not unsurprising that al-Quds was the first *qibla*, or direction of prayer in Islam, before the Ka'ba in Mecca.

Thus when Umar Ibn al-Khattab, the Prophet Muhammad's companion and the second caliph, conquered Jerusalem in 637, he decided on the place for a mosque dedicated to the miraculous night journey. It was precisely around the rock sacred also to Jews, where the two temples were destroyed by the Babylonians and the Romans. The Dome of the Rock was completed and opened in 691. It is the most ancient, majestic mosque, built by Caliph Abd al-Malik Ibn Marwan, not by chance belonging to the Umayyad dynasty, which bequeathed to the world irreplaceable jewels of Islamic architecture.

The Dome of the Rock, therefore, has a unique role in the Muslim religious imagination: the place is full of meaning because the Prophet Muhammad was given the possibility to ascend to heaven, to meet some of the earlier prophets (Abraham, Moses, and Jesus), and then to return to Earth and recount what he saw. For Muslims it validates the bond between the early Islam rooted in the Arabian desert and the Islam of the Levant, as the land of the Abrahamic religions. Jerusalem is thus iconic, although it is not—like Mecca and Medina—the destination of the Hajj, the pilgrimage, the fifth pillar of Islam.

In its inhabitants' popular religiosity, al-Quds is nevertheless tantamount to the first two Islamic cities, as evident from the symbols on the white walls of the houses. It is not the whitish shade of Jerusalem stone that covers some houses in the eastern part of the city. It is instead the white dye painted on outside walls to signify that someone in the family has completed the Hajj to Mecca and Medina. Pilgrims apply stencils to the white walls, making a kind of brightly colored and starry heaven. In the more refined murals dedicated to the Hajj, especially in Egypt, walls become chronicles through naive drawings, like storytellers' vignettes. But Jerusalem graffiti are simpler. On the walls, the unknown artist paints stars, festoons, written well-wishes, and especially images of holy places. It is not only the Ka'ba that is portrayed, that is taken for granted, but also the Dome of the Rock, the intimate holy place, the local measurement of faith.

The Dome of the Rock is iconic for the Muslim faithful. It means almost nothing to Christians, except for evangelical Protestants who would like to replace the Dome of the Rock with the Temple described in the Bible. But it is taboo for Judaism, given that the Dome of the Rock and the nearby al-Aqsa Mosque were built on the Jewish Temple Mount, the place of the Holy of Holies, the wide area of the ancient city of Jerusalem where the First and Second Temple were built and then destroyed. The Dome of the Rock, therefore, is the representation in absentia of the Jewish belonging to Jerusalem: the temple (of another faith) has been built over the known Jewish temple that was destroyed, a physical form that fills the space and the volume of something that used to be. For observant Jews, the Dome of the Rock is a juxtaposition.

Religious conflict, including the confrontation on the Dome of the Rock as a (present or in absentia) icon of faith, represents, however, an immediate reading of what happened in Jerusalem concerning places considered 'holy' by the current religions in the city. It is not a reductive reading, certainly, but it is only one part of the myth of Jerusalem. It constitutes, if anything, the old myth, antique, age-old, well-known, that makes the city the earthly representative of the archetype, the archetype of heavenly Jerusalem. The Holy City often disappointed pilgrims' expectations, as many took the journey believing that they could possess on Earth the marvelous magnitude of the afterlife. In fact, through Jerusalem's different ages, they were faced with a little provincial town, small, even neglected and degraded, and sometimes extremely poor.

Conversely, the contemporary and postmodern myth of Jerusalem is largely the result of a lack of astonishment. Jerusalem is well known. Pilgrims arrive equipped with tourist guides swollen with details, maps, photos, with useful phone directories and erudite descriptions of every single stone in the Old City. They are ready to swallow Jerusalem in a few days, led from one famous place to another, scarcely ever crossing the anonymous streets of the city. There is no longer the surprise of the unknown experienced by the early pilgrims who longed for and idealized the Holy City. Jerusalem was a hidden city, as the first pilgrims set out on foot for the years-long journey of a lifetime, trying to live a complete submersion in faith and, why not, in the world. In those days Jerusalem was a city to explore with an admiring gaze, to be talked about, on their return home, to the bystanders who gathered to listen to the pilgrims.

How distant is today's Jerusalem from its profoundly religious myth? Current categories have less to do with faith and are more mundane, political, nationalistic, and—let's say it—decidedly commercial. As historian Stephen Bennett writes, "in the modern era, the religious myth of Jerusalem became secondary to intra-national and international conflict."[75] Jerusalem's devotional conception bowed down to mass tourism. Furthermore, its tied-in consumerism has succeeded where nothing succeeded for thousands of years, in transforming Jerusalem into a normal or normalized city, and a tourist destination like any other. It also gave rise to Jerusalem's universally recognized logo, reproduced endlessly by the tchotchke and souvenir industry.

The logo par excellence is, precisely, the Dome of the Rock, replicated on tasteless ties, aprons, refrigerator magnets, and key chains, hats, mouse pads, iPad and smartphone covers, eco-friendly cloth bags, posters, and shirts. A mosque, a sacred building, it is the paradoxical tool that transforms holy Jerusalem and its unattainableness into a normal city: the perfect and enticing photo in travel magazines. The result is the dematerialization of the Dome, so that it loses its physicality in favor of its virtual image, reproduced endlessly, visible everywhere, available online. If, as it indisputably is, the Dome of the Rock is a work of art and not merely a place with profound religious significance, it is equally evident that its endless 'reproduction' on the tourist industry's tchotchkes has the power to debase its uniqueness. It deprives tourists and especially pilgrims of the desire to discover what is unknown and only imagined. Walter Benjamin's classic and never outdated definition appears true once more: "What withers in the age of the technological reproducibility of the work of art is the latter's aura." Benjamin's definition also fits perfectly the aura of a monument, of a temple, of a building that is evoked, talked of, described as imposing and incredible, and that instead is reproduced as a mere consumer product. The Dome of the Rock becomes a replica of itself and fully a part of postmodernity: "This process is symptomatic; its significance extends far beyond the realm of art. It might be stated as a general formula that the technology of reproduction detaches the reproduced object from the sphere of tradition."[76]

The golden Dome, ambiguous in being full of religious and political references, is the logo of a city that, looking back at its history, is full of often-conflicting symbols that cannot be synthesized in any monument. However, marketing a city requires that its trademark be unique. The brand of a city must be condensed, almost erasing the complexity of its representation. Very few tourists, *ex abrupto*, would in fact know what the Dome is, what its history is, even what its religious role and significance is. Is it a mosque or merely a monument? Is it a sacred Muslim building, or something else? Only for the inhabitants of Jerusalem does the Dome retain all its physicality, its imposing volume, and, at the same time, its plural significance. It is the Dome whose impressive size threatens even beyond the walls that surround and contain the Old City. As a guardian, it emerges, gleaming and consuming, while Jerusalemites stop at the twenty-four-hour baker's to buy their last items before hurrying home. In the chaotic daily life of Damascus Gate, the somewhat overwhelming structure of the mosque fills everything: the gaze of the inhabitants and of the tourists, the air, the sky. The Dome is a spaceship landed in Jerusalem, an alien object amid the whiteness of the stone, the gray of the asphalt and the pavements, the usual madness of untidily parked cars, traffic lights, and street crossings. And the gilt of the Dome clashes with the pallid white and the gray of the city.

The virtual dimension of the Dome of the Rock, however, is even more hegemonic than its importance for the daily life of Jerusalem. The

Dome of the Rock is like St. Peter's in the souvenir stalls around the Vatican for the mass of Catholic pilgrims. It is the stencil reproduced everywhere, in the little souvenir stores of the Old City and online. It is the infinite reproduction of the logo. If Jerusalem were to lose its supernal aura, the Dome of the Rock would inevitably become 'any' urban icon, just like the Eiffel Tower that contains within itself all the modern complexity of Paris, or the Colosseum that distills the historical stratification and the imperial grandeur of Rome. In its mundane character, the Dome of the Rock is an 'urban icon' that contains everything: faith, Israeli and Palestinian nationalist symbols, conflict, the city divided, and, on the contrary, the city forcibly shared.

(Re)Branding Jerusalem

Even the Israeli Tourist Ministry has chosen the Dome of the Rock as its icon of Jerusalem. At first sight, the choice might appear paradoxical. The ideas that underlie the use of the Dome of the Rock in the promotional presentations of the Tourist Ministry are, undoubtedly, the *loss* and the *absence*. For the tourist imagination, and especially for Jewish pilgrims, what is important in the picture is what is missing: there is the loss of the Second Temple, destroyed by Titus, and there is the absence of the third temple that will one day be built, when God determines. And yet today there are mosques, the Noble Sanctuary, on the Temple Mount. But, the Israeli radical settlers and the fundamentalist Jews and Christians say, it is only a historical time, a present time that will end.

Notwithstanding, Jerusalem is not only its urban logo. It is also the logo of Israel that wants to be like any normal country, like Thailand for example: a tourist attraction like so many others, without a sign of conflict. In recent years, the Israeli advertisement machine has tried to portray Jerusalem as a normal holiday destination, as if the Israeli–Palestinian conflict were interiorized and transformed into a component of Israel's national history. Nir Barkat explained this with obvious pride in a public interview in the Grand Synagogue of Jerusalem. "We've convinced the national government that the brand 'Jerusalem' is stronger than the brand 'Israel,'" he said to his interviewer, David Horovitz, in February 2013. Then so as not to leave any room for a different interpretation, the

Israeli mayor of Jerusalem entered into specifics: "If you want to get tourists to Israel, you'd better focus on the brand 'Jerusalem.' A lot of people don't even know that Jerusalem is in Israel. They ask me, 'When I travel, is Jerusalem next to Israel somehow?'"[77]

Barkat, a secular Israeli who surprisingly won a difficult electoral campaign in 2008 against the orthodox Meir Porush, relied on numbers for his explanation. According to the Tourism Ministry's official statistics, 3.5 million visitors came to Israel in 2012, 4 percent more than the previous year. A record was broken, and, what is more significant, it confirmed the upward trend that started in 2006, after the end of the al-Aqsa Intifada. During the long years of the Palestinian revolt (2001–2005) and the tragic waves of suicide attacks on Jerusalem's public transportation and leisure hotspots, the city emptied out, as the international tourism industry almost canceled it from the list of destinations. Left alone by pilgrims, the city returned to its provincial dimensions and its name became equivalent to terror and blood. The trend's reversal since 2006 has meant a renewed crescendo of tourists for Jerusalem, undeterred by the 'low intensity' conflict in the West Bank or the intermittent Israeli military operations against Gaza.

A tour to Israel necessarily means a visit to Jerusalem, either for faith or 'simple' tourism. For the aseptic lexicon of marketing, Jerusalem is Israel's brand: the sacred magnet, the magnet that certainly attracts Jewish pilgrims. For each, the city is the ethno-religious goal and will always remain "next year in Jerusalem"—*hashana haba'a b'Yrushalayim*—as recited in the Seder, the Jewish Easter feast. According to cold statistics, however, it is Christian pilgrims, especially Russians, who constantly fill the hotels of the city in an exponential crescendo, especially through the connections with Moscow cultivated by Stas Misezhnikov, the dynamic minister of tourism in Benjamin Netanyahu's government from 2009 to the elections of 2013.

Faithful Jews and Christian pilgrims: Israel's tourism strategy in recent years has focused on these two well-defined groups. In fact, for most Muslims there are two kinds of restrictions. There is the aggressive Israeli mistrust that underlies the stringent—and often humiliating—security controls applied to the few Arab travelers, either those of Arab origin or even those with a name that could be linked to Muslim tradition. There is also the restriction Arabs and non-Arab Muslims place on themselves, based on boycotting Jerusalem as a pilgrimage destination as part of not recognizing the political and military control of the city by the Israelis. They do not boycott the religious character of Jerusalem, they boycott the political context, that is, the occupation. They prefer to sacrifice the pilgrimage to the "furthest Mosque" on the altar of the conflict's paradigms from 1967 onward: better not to visit the paths trodden by the prophet Issa (the Arab name of Jesus) or the Tomb of Ibrahim (the Arab name of Abraham) in an otherwise tortured city like Hebron, the Palestinian Khalil.

Until now, there has been little new in the Israeli tourism strategy for Jerusalem, no tangible sign of discontinuity with respect to the image the city has had for centuries. It is now as it used to be in early times the destination of an exclusively religious pilgrimage that has been translated according to different tourist vocabularies. In Crusader times, the medieval pilgrimage ran parallel to the military campaigns. During the nineteenth and twentieth centuries, the few and in some ways elitist travelers tried to rediscover the Bible in the Holy Land as seen especially through British eyes, thus strengthening European orientalism.

The Israeli establishment, however, has not fenced itself into maintaining or even promoting more energetically what Barkat called the Jerusalem brand. It has pursued a real and true 'rebranding' operation, as advertisers and marketing experts would say. Rebranding means remodeling Israel's image, of which tourism is a fundamental part. It is, to be honest, one of the pillars of a far from hidden strategy, and has been generally known since 2005, when the Brand Israel project began. The declared objective was to transform the international image of Israel, a country permanently at war, a tough country, militaristic, even a macho one. There had to be a different image. Israel had to become the technologically advanced country, where—in addition to Jerusalem—there is also Tel Aviv. With its long beach and its secular flavor, Tel Aviv acquired the label of a city that is respectful of civil rights, open and aggressive.

The distance between Jerusalem and Tel Aviv is actually part of the Israeli tourist strategy. The Tourism Ministry, basically, has done nothing to mitigate the dissonance of the imagery—especially locally, as well as internationally—between a city that is confined in its stereotyping image (Jerusalem) and a city that stretches toward the future (Tel Aviv). It makes use of a real dichotomy between the two cities that serves, if anything, to show that in Israel there is everything. There is Jerusalem the pious, devout, the Holy City. And then there is the ill repute of Tel Aviv, a city that comes alive at night, an Israeli hotspot with a lot of American flavor.

Nir Barkat, however, goes further. He makes it clear that the Israeli brand's transformation should also include Jerusalem. He is the mayor with a persona to embody the discontinuity, from the uncritical stereotype of the pious and devoted Jerusalem to the manifold, also secular Israeli city. Barkat's aim is clear: with lots of initiatives, he wants to eclipse the gray period of his predecessor, the orthodox Uri Lupolianski, the symbol of a city along the lines of the ultra-orthodox community that is in an unstoppable demographic expansion.

Barkat's activism was obvious from the first moment, as the city began to attract conventions and sports events (from a temporary ice rink to marathons). In June 2013, the municipality hosted a Formula One car race called "Formula Jerusalem—A Peace Journey," which triggered severe reactions among Palestinians. Barkat's idea is that there is another Jerusalem, and that if it becomes fossilized beneath its religious dimensions it would be deprived of many of its Israeli inhabitants, as has happened in recent years with the exodus of secular people, especially the young, toward suburbs to the north of the city. And so it emerges that Jerusalem's sanctity is a brand to be sold like any other product. In this case, it serves to attract pilgrims, but especially tourists who could then experience the city in its entire cultural dimension. Hence a mundane city.

Look at the recent direction in architecture in the commercial area of Jerusalem. Mamilla, just outside Jaffa Gate, is precisely the main destination for tourism, primarily Jewish—especially American—even more than Dung Gate, which leads to the Western Wall. Mamilla, the ancient Ma'man Allah, was the most important and historical Muslim cemetery of the city. The cemetery is now reduced to a forgotten and neglected place next to (and under) the building site of the planned Museum of Tolerance, a highly debated and controversial Simon Wiesenthal Center project. In present-day Jerusalem, Mamilla is synonymous with elegance and shopping. It has the highest concentration of five-star hotels, which has transformed it into Jerusalem's most fashionable area, especially for travelers.

The story of the Mamilla project is illustrative of the debate that for decades has involved not just Israeli architects but also city planners, legislators, and politicians. It is also a living example of the fact that architecture in post-1967 Jerusalem has never been neutral, not even today. The debate started with urban planning for what was a no-man's-land from 1948 to 1967, along the walls of Suleiman the Magnificent leading to Jaffa Gate. From the Six-Day War until today, Jaffa Gate is the entrance to the ancient Jewish quarter. Pilgrims and tourists start their visit at the Tower of David, just inside Jaffa Gate, where they are told the history of the indissoluble link between the kingdom of David and Israel before being directed along the walls to reach the Western Wall in what was once the Mughrabi quarter, cleaned up and redesigned (at least originally) by Moshe Safdie.

Outside the Old City, not far from Jaffa Gate, lies the cozy quarter of Yemin Moshe, the dream of Sir Moses Montefiore, and at the back there is the King David Hotel, no longer the heart of the British Mandate but instead the visitor's ticket to the new Israel that won back Jerusalem. From Jaffa Gate to the western petit-bourgeois residential districts stretches an area that for years and years held the attention of town planners. It has been named after the Muslim cemetery: Mamilla, Ma'man Allah.

Nestled in the planners' secular renewal concept, the Mamilla project has seen in recent years an acceleration that has changed the very heart of Jerusalem. The long stretch of buildings from the David Citadel Hotel to Jaffa Gate indicates a turning point from a city planning perspective. In Ottoman times and during the British Mandate, the commercial avenue that led to Jaffa Gate wound along the walls, serving as an extended market. The ancient walls that led to Jaffa Gate were not a focal point, as they are today, because the Old City, the Tower of David, and Jaffa Gate are the goal, the end point of the boulevard that nowadays crosses Mamilla. Planners were likely inspired by American models, such as the broad avenues of Washington, DC.

The ambiance of the hotel that stretches toward the ancient walls is New York-ish. And so is the hotel's roof garden, where sails are unfurled over the guests' heads to protect them from the evening humidity or from the scorching sun of the nearby desert. The terrace of the Mamilla Hotel is like the prow of a cruise ship approaching the treasures of the tour: a prow that skirts Jaffa Gate, the skillfully illuminated walls, the postcard Jerusalem. It is no ordinary hotel, and not just because it was designed by Moshe Safdie, one of the most important architects in the world, nor because the interior is by a well-known designer, Piero Lissoni. Far more than this, the Mamilla Hotel is the diamond-point in one of the longest-debated urban planning projects of post-1967 Jerusalem. In fact, it is the longest since the times of Teddy Kollek, the man who actually determined the face of the present city.

The Mamilla Hotel is the gate to an open-air mall, the latest hangout. It is truly a hodgepodge of cafes and mid-range stores, franchises, and small Israeli fashion outlets, almost a separate world to relax in without religious buildings, ancient stones, tour guides, and religious stalls, as in the best mass tourist tradition. Thus Mamilla fills the gap that always existed in Jerusalem: a commercial area that, before the opening of the mall on the fringes of the Old City, was always represented by Jaffa Street. As a long artery for dirt-cheap shopping, Jaffa Street stretched from the ancient walls to the traditional market of Mahane Yehuda, far in the northern suburbs. In recent Jerusalemite memory, nevertheless, Jaffa Street incarnates the sorrowful image of the most frightening suicide attacks that have rocked the city. On the contrary, Mamilla embodies the desire of the municipal (and national) authorities to change the brand of Jerusalem. The intention is to make the city, in its own image, a destination that is much closer to the urban realities sought after with mass tourism. Israel acts as if Jerusalem were simply as pictured in its glamourous brochures: peaceful, reconciled, united. Normalized.

However, it is more than difficult, it is almost impossible to separate Jerusalem from its iconic past and present. The city is its logo. Jerusalem's complicated sacredness has always been its brand and will always remain so. Jerusalem is the Holy City, the way Paris is the City of Lights and New York is the Big Apple. Without the holy there would be no city, Jerusalem. Its secular dimension is only an accessory, when it is not at risk of being an alibi and of veiling the true secular dimension of the city: conflict, division, the plurality of its belonging. Avishai Margalit, one of the most important Israeli philosophers, has described the unhappy destiny of Jerusalem and its myth as even more terrible. "The Holy City is indeed a place fraught with ambivalence," he wrote, "on the one hand it contains a divine presence that provides it with an abundance of goodness; on the other hand, there is a constant danger of defilement that will alienate the divinity and threaten the city with a curse. This ambivalence between goodness and evil, love and fear, and especially purity and defilement, produces the religious tension expressed in the idea of the Temple as a place that is at once blessed and dangerous."[78]

Al-Aqsa Graffiti

The vessel has a broad outline, so broad as to be able to contain the Dome of the Rock, a significant metaphor for Jerusalem, and as a consequence an allegory for historical Palestine. The stormy waters endanger the ship, which nevertheless continues on its way to salvation. The brilliant colors hide the miserable condition of the wall on which the mural has been painted, one of many that define the myth of Jerusalem in the heart of Gaza City.

For the Palestinians who live, suffer, and die in Gaza, Jerusalem is the unattainable goal. It is the heart of Palestinian identity, from which they are separated by the conflict, and by the Separation Wall built by the Israelis to close off the Strip. Even in Gaza, as in so many places where the Palestinian people have been split up, Jerusalem is the icon of identity, and once again the Dome of the Rock is its logo. Jerusalem is in the suitcase that every Palestinian carries, together with the *keffiyeh*, the Palestinian flag, and the key of the house that was left in haste when they were driven out. They are all symbols of a 'virtual nation'[79] created over decades by the diaspora and kept alive by the diaspora through a visual management of symbols. In Gaza City, in the refugee camps in Lebanon and Syria, in the vast and liquid e-nation, there is also an electronic and virtual Palestine: graphics, photo collections, logos, both on and through the web. The 'virtual nation' emerges also through songs as a texture of poetry and music—now considered classic hits, not only for Palestinian nationalism but even for the whole of pan-Arabism.

Hence it is not possible to think of Jerusalem as the symbol of the Palestinian nation without listening to songs such as *Zahrat al-mada'in*, "Flower of Cities," and *al-Quds al-'atiqa*, better known as "al-Quds in My Heart," a nationalistic mantra on the radio and on YouTube. These are the songs that have made Fayrouz an irreplaceable myth, as she is not only a Lebanese singer but also a musical icon throughout the Middle East. If Fayrouz is in the Middle East musical hall of fame due to what seems an outdated political song, it is still true that Jerusalem continues to be the unforgettable theme, even in musical expressions that at first sight seem far from a classical imprint. The time of exile is different today from yesterday. Political song has given way to an intimacy that did not exist before. Yet, Jerusalem is still there, as a heart-breaking memory of the exiles' origins. "It has melted all the names in my blood/Jerusalem, the kiss of Jerusalem/Now I am a wandering planet/In a distant universe/In a strange time," sings Nabil Salameh, the singer of Radiodervish, a well-known world music band based in Italy. Salameh, a Palestinian born in Tripoli, Lebanon, and originally from Jaffa, was able to wander the city thanks to his Italian citizenship. He wandered through Jerusalem always with the feeling of being illegal in his own country. His song *Ainaki* is the outcome not only of his longing for Jerusalem but also of a generational shift in conceptualizing exile.

However, it is on a tiny piece of land known as the Gaza Strip where the Palestinian myth of Jerusalem shows all its complexity. It is a symbol that embodies religious, nationalist, identity-based, emotional, even martial elements all at the same time. Through the recurring depiction of the Dome of the Rock, more than of al-Aqsa Mosque, the presence of Jerusalem is pervasive.

Jerusalem is iterative in the graffiti that cover the peeled walls along the sidewalks of Gaza City, or rather along the streets that connect the refugee camps, neighborhoods, and villages. The Holy City is an equally constant presence in the iconography of martyrdom. In the endless sequence of huge photographs and graffiti that display the *shahid*, the martyr killed in an Israeli attack often holds a machine gun and a copy of the Quran in his hands, and in the background political figures, Yasser Arafat or Sheikh Ahmed Yassin, are depicted together with the ever-displayed Dome of the Rock. Even graffiti in praise of Hamas fighters, the Ezzedeen al-Qassam Brigade, portray the Dome of the Rock as a logo of Jerusalem, often within the borders of historical Palestine.

Al-Quds is about a hundred kilometers away, but it appears to the inhabitants of Gaza otherworldly, as if it were the heavenly Jerusalem. It is not only the high cement wall built by the Israelis, and especially the tight blockade that has locked up the Strip for the last decade, that separates the bare, dusty streets of Gaza City, Rafah, and Jabaliya from the Holy City. History unfolded independently in the enclaves that fragmented the Palestinian landscape. Gaza, the West Bank, the consistent community of Palestinians who remained in the pre-1948 areas, all these virtual and/or de facto enclaves followed different historical paths. So has Jerusalem: due to events from 1948 on, the Holy City has been distanced from the rest of the Palestinian territory. Hence Gaza and Jerusalem are distant from each other because they have lived separately for so many years that their different historical paths mark a distance in their very identities.

As occurred among the Palestinian diaspora in Lebanon, Syria, and Jordan, Jerusalem's myth replaced the reality in Gaza. Jerusalem as the symbol of Palestinian religious and national identity enshrouds the city as a physical place. Moreover, for the younger generation that has never had or even requested a permit from the Israeli authorities to visit Jerusalem, the city is nothing more than what appears in Gaza iconography: photographs, graffiti, murals, objects. Above all, Jerusalem's myth has been fed by family oral history: tales of parents, grandparents, ancestors describe Jerusalem as a place that no longer exists. The city of their memories is nestled in pre-1948 Palestine, when Jerusalem was quite a small city and did not contain—as it contains today—almost nine hundred thousand inhabitants. In family stories Jerusalem is no more than a place of origin, talked about with the nostalgia that consumes emigrants (in this case refugees, forced to leave their homes during the first Arab–Israeli war). Jerusalem is the Dome of the Rock embroidered by mothers and draped over the good sofas. It is al-Aqsa Mosque reproduced on a large ceramic plate. It is the large poster hung on the office wall that shows the whole of the Noble Sanctuary and celebrates the day when it will return into the hands of the Palestinians. It is the Dome of the Rock on the prayer rug put on the shoulders of the faithful while they approach the mosque, or left on a chair, waiting to be used for the *salah*. Jerusalem is the enormous photograph dominating public offices, or behind the desk of a Hamas leader, together with the Palestinian flag. It is the reproduction of the Dome of the Rock on the label of a decoration, or on a kitschy wooden souvenir exposed on a little table in the living room.

Every icon, whether for tourist consumption or identity-related, needs its tchotchke industry. The Palestinian 'icon market' speaks the language of nostalgia. Jerusalem, in Gaza as in the refugee camps outside the borders of Israel/Palestine, is the nation that no longer exists, the lost land, the broken history.

Al-Quds al-Arabi, the Holy City of the Arabs

There is another myth of Jerusalem, different from that of the Palestinians. It is an even more widespread and pervasive myth pertaining to the Arab region as a whole, and stretching to the much wider and multifaceted Muslim world. The distinction is inevitable. The myth of Jerusalem, or rather of al-Quds, is different depending on the latitude and distance from the Holy City. Al-Quds as a cultural and political myth varies in Amman and Jakarta, despite the fact that the Holy City's political connotation and religious meaning are similar in Amman and in Jakarta. Amman's involvement is profoundly different, and goes beyond the very imposing presence of the Palestinian population in Jordan. Al-Quds affects the Jordanian identity as a whole. The Dome of the Rock as the logo on the front door of al-Quds Restaurant in Amman, in other words, refers the clientele or passersby to a local historical and human geography composed of journeys, family connections, and social relations that have existed over centuries.

Monotonously, overwhelmingly, repetitively, the logo inundates the streets of Amman, Cairo, Beirut, Damascus. In each and every case, the Dome of the Rock is the timely reminder of a flesh-and-bone city, of a religious identity, and of a political goal. The "tomorrow, at al-Quds" of pan-Arabism.

Al-Quds is a myth and a logo. It is also a tool of pressure and influence that brings together all the protagonists of Arab politics, even in acts that may at first glance seem far from the halls of power. One of the last architectural mega-projects approved at Doha by Sheikh Hamad bin Khalifa al-Thani was called, and not by chance, al-Quds Endowment Tower. This is the name given to the over hundred-story skyscraper whose foundations were laid in 2009. Planned as a multifunctional center, al-Quds Tower in its very conception shows how much the Dome of the Rock remains the unrivalled logo of Jerusalem. The logo is reiterated in fact endlessly, repeated in the golden domes that—hypertrophic—appear in the winning project of an international architectural competition by Omar Elfar, a young Egyptian architect working for the Arab Engineering Bureau in Qatar. The reference is clear. It is in fact programmatic in the Tower's name and in the project's design. Arab collective imagination needs to confirm its support for Jerusalem, not just by politics but also through contemporary forms.

Politics has its own tools, then, such as those used by the emir of Qatar over the years. It was not by chance that the first stone of al-Quds Tower was put in place by the Palestinian prime minister at that time, Ismail Haniyeh, one of the most important leaders of Hamas in the Gaza Strip. To some extent the most theatrical act, however, was performed precisely by the Qatari emir at the summit meeting of the Arab League in March 2013 in Doha, at which he established a fund of $1 billion to protect the Arab and Islamic cultural heritage of Jerusalem. A billion dollars, one-quarter given by the Qatar Emirate, challenged Israel and the idea that Jerusalem is only Israeli and only Jewish. In this emphatic way, Qatar was also giving a hard response to what happened in 2009, when celebrations for Jerusalem as the 'capital of Arab culture' were not only forbidden but directly opposed, in East Jerusalem, by the Israeli authorities.

In the Arab world, the reiteration of the name al-Quds in every context is so overabundant, long-lasting, in a way endless as to have almost lost connection with the real city. It is practically impossible to make an exhaustive directory of businesses—cafes, restaurants, inns, supermarkets, food shops—named al-Quds in every Arab country. Likewise, an endless series of these shops display the Dome of the Rock as an icon. And finally, a similar number of newspapers, television programs, foundations, and charities recall Jerusalem in their name, transforming al-Quds from a city to a political banner under which Arab regimes have often hidden other goals, whether national or regional.

5

JERUSALEM ONE AND SHARED

The fact is that you are a stranger, as
Jews are strangers in the rest of
the diaspora. Teaching you Hebrew I
am preparing you to emigrate to
the Land of Israel.

—Sami Michael, "Victoria"[80]

You are still dreaming
On the wall of this city
Like a bird
Chasing the migrant summer
Our time is a tale
Where we have become
The eternal exile.

—Nabil Salameh, lyrics, "City Lights"

I n Europe, the 'two-state solution' is the only firm point in which
to believe for anyone who wishes for peace between Israelis and
Palestinians: two states for two peoples, one beside the other in peace
and security, with a divided Jerusalem as capital for both Israelis and
Palestinians. It is Oslo's "mantra," the mystical formula, used in all the

meetings and conferences, as if it were innate, inherent in the Israeli–Palestinian conflict. A sacred, untouchable expression, a certainty and at the same time a balm for international public opinion that seeks remedies. Whether the remedies are feasible or not is another story. Oslo's mantra is untouchable, and he or she who dares to call it into question is considered a staunch adversary of peace between Israelis and Palestinians.

The problem is that the process, or the plan, formulated during the Oslo negotiations and blessed by President Bill Clinton in the Rose Garden at the White House on September 13, 1993, succeeded in uniting three weaknesses. First, it is unrealized. Second, it is not feasible in practice, given what has taken place between then and today. And third, since the beginning, its gradualism hid what today, some twenty years later, is completely manifest. The goal pursued by at least one of the parties involved, namely, Israel, through actions taken by all the governments, was a never-ending status quo. In fact, a permanent state of transition allowed Israelis to build colonies in most of the West Bank, and to a lesser degree in Gaza, at least until the unilateral disengagement carried out by Israel in August 2005. The international community did not seriously impede what was and is a very clear political plan for the Israelis. For their part, Palestinians opposed in specific periods the patent violation of the Oslo peace agreement using the abominable and counterproductive tool of terrorism.

There is only one inevitable conclusion resulting from this state of affairs: the two-state solution is impossible to put into practice, has no relation to reality, and shows no understanding of the situation on the ground, least of all in Jerusalem.

Jerusalem cannot be divided. And it cannot divide itself. This is not because the enforced unification of 1967, carried out by Israel in the Six-Day War, was the solution to the conflict. The problem, in fact, does not date from 1967. The unresolved crux actually stems from 1948, and from the armistice line that divided the city.

After the failure of the Oslo paradigm, the idea of Jerusalem as *corpus separatum*—a crucial component of the United Nations partition plan—is becoming topical again. And there is nothing paradoxical in it. Jerusalem is one city, a single urban body, an ancient and stratified structure that cannot be divided either on a map or physically. It cannot, however, be unified and administered by just one of the parties at war, because this unification *by force* does not resolve the conflict nor address the need for justice that alone can make the peace a long-lasting one.

So what now? As Jerusalem's destiny cannot be anchored to only one party's perspective, that the city is the unique capital of the state of Israel, eternal and indivisible. As Jerusalem cannot be simply al-Quds, the capital of Palestine. If the city cannot be, in reality and in the respect owed to its history and its inhabitants, divided into two parts, then what possible solution can there be that is dignified and just for all its inhabitants?

It is neither wise nor serious to think of having a solution in hand. No one in the last century has had one. One thing is beyond doubt: the city nowadays is not any more at the disposal of the powers beyond and within the confines of Israel/Palestine. Jerusalem is its inhabitants, the people in its streets. Their sons and descendants, they belong to the city. And the city, inevitably, belongs first and foremost to them. To them only.

The reality on the ground, the most recent facts confirm the understanding of Jerusalem as a city that cannot be normalized by force. Any solution worthy of the name must be based on a pillar without which all political–diplomatic structures are destined to implode. The pillar is reciprocal recognition. The noun 'recognition' was included in the Oslo mantra, and in the semantic apparatus in use in the last twenty years, marked by the paradigm of the two-state solution. The difference here rests entirely in the adjective that stands beside it: 'reciprocal.' Reciprocity clarifies that there cannot be one homologous Jerusalem, identitarian, ethnically pure or cleansed, by either party. There cannot be a solely Israeli and a solely Jewish Jerusalem, or a Jerusalem administered, controlled, managed solely by the Israeli authorities. At the same time, there will never be, not even in the dreams of the Muslim and the Christian fundamentalist fringe, a single Palestinian Jerusalem, only Arab, organized according to two religions: Islam and Christianity.

This seems obvious and banal, if not disrespectful toward the international elites' cleverness—such pretentious elucidation, a useless, pleonastic explanation. Whoever has lived in Jerusalem and knows the details of its complexity and the difficulty of its daily life knows that the very idea of reciprocity cannot be taken for granted. And yet the reality is in the cohabitation, in an often forced co-existence, between the two communities, Israeli and Palestinian. It is a daily fact, clearly visible in the life of the city, in the physical use of the city, in the current customs of the city. But reciprocity is something else: its meaning digs deeper into respect for the 'other,' into a relation between two peoples and two communities that is anchored in sharing. Two individuals, two communities, each recognizes the reciprocal history in the city, the reciprocal attachment to Jerusalem. Each recognizes to the other the reciprocal love of the place itself, which comes from history, memory, identity. Each recognizes even the other's cultural and physical possession and, in a way, the proprietorship of the city: it is possession, it is ownership that overlaps at times, at other times is communal, and at other times still is stratified, like puff pastry, impossible to subdivide precisely. Otherwise, the result would be only one: the whole construction would crumble.

According to this idea of 'one and shared' Jerusalem, the city is considered in its urban uniqueness, without detaching the so-called Holy Basin, the Old City and the surrounding areas with their exceptional patrimony of holy places, from the rest of the present-day city. Its actual, complex structure has to embrace the ancient historical center and the middle-class districts just outside the ancient walls of Suleiman the Magnificent, up even to the suburbs and the settlements constructed more recently. It would include the multifaceted urban reality produced by the political–administrative facts on the ground. For better or worse, Jerusalem nowadays includes the new residential districts that Teddy Kollek decided to create in order to Israelize the city and, in parallel, the Palestinian suburbs developed by way of impressive demographic pressure during the 1980s and 1990s. Jerusalem is the massive Israeli settlements on the city's outskirts, to the south and to the north, and the Palestinian districts that are now on the other side of the Separation Wall.

The Holy Basin is surely the core of the Jerusalem problem. At the same time, it is not possible today to separate the Old City from the rest of

Jerusalem's urban dimension. The inhabited area around the various sacred buildings has been for millennia 'the city'—the city in its entirety. In the last hundred and fifty years, however, it has been transformed into a part for the whole, into a synecdoche, a sign, or more plainly into the historical center of an ever more complex and vast agglomeration. It is impossible therefore to define a destiny for the Old City different from that of the whole of Jerusalem, as envisioned in the abundant plans for the international administration of the holy places. The Old City is not the Vatican of the Three Faiths. Nothing could be more unimaginable, not only because it would be unfeasible but also—above all—because the Old City and the new Jerusalem are the same thing. They are two parts of the same structure, broader and more complicated than before. They are two organs—by now on the same decisive level—of a machine that cannot function without either. As the heart of Jerusalem, therefore, the Old City cannot be removed from the political solution, as if it were a foreign body.

Simply considering the holy places, now contained and identified in the Old City, as an integral and component part of the city in its municipal boundaries (to be redesigned yet again), it is possible to think of a shared urban reality.

It must not be treated like the Vatican or like a museum of the faiths, or as on par with Ayutthaya, the city of a hundred temples, the heart of Siamese spirituality. The Old City of Jerusalem should be consigned to its historical dimension, to which the holy places belong, if they are not to be treated like a Disneyland of the monotheistic religions but rather consigned to the heart of our anthropological culture, as Mediterranean peoples. This is the reason why this book has assumed the weight of a title so contradictory and paradoxical, *Jerusalem without God*. It is not, nor does it want to be, a trial balloon, an easy provocation before a city that, on the contrary, needs to regain its humanity (and therefore its dignity) in order to be able to retrieve its God, according to the three religions of the Book.

It is not by chance that in recent years anyone who has given thought to a shared solution that goes further than Oslo has come across minor difficulties concerning Jerusalem, in thinking about the city's future. Many more and bigger difficulties are involved in trying to combine—in a full and complete geographic dimension—identity and cohabitation, security in its own future as a community and belonging to the small, same, common land. In short, it is difficult to think of a destiny shared by Israel and Palestine, without hard, careful, long cultural and moral work in order to understand that the land between the Mediterranean and the river Jordan is an integral part of the identity of both. The problem—if anything—is how to translate a common belonging into political and institutional terms.

How to explain the indissolubility of a 'common' destiny on the 'common' land of Israelis and Palestinians? Both are legitimate heirs, and a notary is needed to work out the formal question of succession without, however, cutting into the legitimacy of the heir living on the contested and common land, or of those who wish to return and live on that land—in other words Palestinian refugees. And because history is not made of 'ifs' but of reality on the ground, there are also the settlements to consider. Certainly one cannot consider Palestinian refugees and Israeli settlers equal, but peace needs grievous compromises that safeguard, somehow, dignity and justice. If it is impossible to think about the evacuation of the Israeli settlements in the West Bank, if it is impossible to think of rescinding the link between Judaism and biblical sites that are now situated, on contemporary maps, in the West Bank, it is equally impossible to think of a peace that continues to put away in a drawer the fundamental question of Palestinian refugees and their indisputable right of return.

A lasting peace can only be realized on the day when the 'right of return' is accepted not only by Palestinians when speaking of the Jewish people's ancestral link with the promised land, but also by Israelis in recognizing the profound Palestinian connection to the land of which they have been a part and where they have lived for thousands of years. For Palestinian identity, Haifa, Jaffa, 'Akka, Safed are places of their own history that cannot be rewritten at the whim of the conqueror. For the Palestinians it is indissoluble, before as today, the connection with a beloved land, lived in, cultivated, despite being considered by the prevailing narrative and the false *vulgata* uninhabited land and uncared for prior to the arrival of Zionist immigrants.

From this point of view, Jerusalem represents the impossibility of the division. It is foolish to think that the city could be considered one, united by the Israelis. It is equally foolish to think that for the Palestinians Jerusalem is only the small sector to the east of the Green Line, and that the districts of middle-class Palestinian expansion toward the west and the sea (Musrara, Talbiyah, Qatamun, and so forth) are not a part of it. So? From both the theoretical and cultural point of view, the remedy is as simple as it is revolutionary: Jerusalem should be one and shared. That is, it should remain united and should be shared, one city for two communities.

This is the message that in more recent times has arisen in some Israeli and Palestinian intellectual circles—people and groups who in various ways have been reflecting on something that goes beyond the two alternatives proposed so far, namely the two-state solution and the one-state solution. Behind the scenes, in Israel/Palestine and elsewhere, the ranks of the 'beyond Oslo' community are growing. More than a major point in any peace negotiation, Jerusalem is for this community the potential and real laboratory. The thinking is increasingly of Jerusalem as an open city, united, without internal limits, the capital of two states; a city, however, with a special statute, like Brussels for example, with a mayor elected by all the inhabitants (Israeli and Palestinian, without distinction) and equal representation for the two constituencies in the communal government.

The model of separation does not work for the Jerusalem observed, conceived, imagined by these circles, composed of politicians, intellectuals, activists, Israeli and Palestinian men and women who live on the 'common land' and at times have undertaken a difficult and extremely frank dialogue. Not only because the demographic and geographic realities created by Israel in its governance of the city have made separation impossible, but also because the importance, and the religious and internal sacredness, of the city drive in only one direction. Jerusalem must remain open, beyond the various walls that now close or wound it.

Several genuine bases for discussion have intensified dialogue in these circles since 2013. One concerns Jerusalem itself, defined as a capital of two states, a "united city, communal and open to the citizens of the two states," for which "there would be established a special municipal government under shared rule and with equal participation on the part of the two peoples," Israeli and Palestinian. "The borders of Jerusalem," continues the document at the base of the dialogue, conceived as a joint work, "would be based on the borders of the Israeli and Jordanian city of 1967, with necessary modifications. The holy places of the Christians, Muslims and Jews would be under international control."

An open city, united but above all shared—this is the heart of the idea, a single urban reality, whose boundaries, however, require reflection. The very definition of Jerusalem's borders is, in fact, part of its future. The idea of the "Two States, One Homeland" initiative, born in 2013 from a series of meetings between Israeli journalist Meron Rapoport and Palestinian political activist Awni al-Mashni, is that the area of the city should be redesigned in such a way as to include all those suburbs, quarters, residential districts that gravitate toward Jerusalem and make up the city. There are some very diverse suburbs among them, and their formal incorporation into Jerusalem would cause many to turn up their noses. To be perfectly clear and specific, one shared Jerusalem would include Maaleh Adumim, the first Israeli settlement transformed into a municipality as an offshoot of Jerusalem, and, by the same title, Abu Dis and Azzariyah, Palestinian villages that currently find themselves beyond the Separation Wall. A 'one and shared' Jerusalem would have to include the Israeli quarters to the northeast, considered by the United Nations to be colonies in the occupied part of the city, that is, Pisgat Zeev, Ramot, Neve Yaakov, and even Gilo, the settlement created between Bethlehem and Jerusalem. In the same way Jerusalem would include Qalandya, considered part of the city before the Wall was constructed.

According to the idea of a 'one and shared' Jerusalem, the entire mosaic of historical quarters, settlements, suburbs, the Old City, and the holy places must represent a single urban body in which there is complete freedom of movement. A city administrated by a shared municipal government, elected by the citizens who reside there, whether Israeli or Palestinian, far from the actual political and administrative model and at the same time far from the idea of an international administration of Jerusalem. The difficulties and obstacles to an idea of this kind are enormous, and some consider them insurmountable at first glance. There are difficulties that, far from being details, represent the terrain against which solutions of this kind must be measured. It is easier, in other words, to think of a solution that cuts, separates, and divides the two communities. It is much more difficult to reflect on questions such as whether Israelis and Palestinians could have joint sovereignty over the great Jerusalem, because the knot of transferring sovereignty is dependent on what, at first sight, seems impossible to put into practice.

Unrealistic, utopian, ingenuous: these are the predictable reactions to such a powerful idea. History has accustomed us to controversies and conflicts that are written and ruled by the winners. This is an indisputable fact, whose unwritten rule finds precisely a breach in the Israeli–Palestinian conflict. Has normalization occurred in Jerusalem? Indeed. Yet at the same time Jerusalem is under a partial and fragile normalization. The potential for a normalized status quo to be broken sooner or later is constant. There is no long-term normalization in sight, as confirmed by the most recent crisis, which the analyst would define as low-intensity conflict. Whoever has lived in Jerusalem would instead consider such a crisis the first sign of civil war. A Jerusalemite civil war.

The idea of a city undivided and shared by its inhabitants springs exactly from the utter awareness of what takes place in the city. Daily life is in fact the primary indication that Jerusalem cannot be divided or, by the same token, be under occupation for a consistent portion of its surface and population. It is a status quo that can last—even for an indeterminate amount of time—but that brings neither peace nor reconciliation nor justice. Nor does it lead, over time, to definitive normalization.

Whoever considers a solution different to the Oslo paradigm or the one-state option also understands very well the complexity of the idea of a Jerusalem one and shared. There are two incontrovertible historical facts, however. The first: for three thousand years until today, Jerusalem has been one. The second: the city has been a laboratory for every sort of idea that has come to light and spread throughout the world. Thus, there is no obstacle to the possibility that the city—even in such a miserable situation—might become yet another singular laboratory for innovative ideas on questions of sovereignty, citizenship, and national identity. The question of Jerusalem speaks about sharing a common land that goes beyond the concept of the frontier, as a recognized border that contains the data of the cultural, communal, and even religious identity.

Jerusalem is one because its identity is composed of historical layers and of men and women who belong to diverse communities. Jerusalem cannot be divided because it is multiple. Jerusalem cannot be made sacred because it is made of flesh and blood inhabitants. Further than the faiths, a Jerusalem without God lives its daily drama. To this city, few unfortunately give heed.

—Jerusalem and Sambuca di Sicilia, Italy, January 2017

NOTES

1   Fadwa El Guindi, *By Noon Prayer: The Rhythm of Islam* (Oxford: Berg, 2007), 153.
2   Quoted in Marc Augé, *Non-Places: Introduction to an Anthropology of Supermodernity*, trans. John Howe (London: Verso, 1992), 77.
3   Ivo Andrić, *The Damned Yard and Other Stories* (London: Forest Books, 1992), 118. Andrić describes in this way the articulated times of the other faiths present in Sarajevo: "The clock on the Catholic cathedral strikes the hour with weighty confidence: 2 a.m. More than a minute passes (to be exact, seventy-five seconds—I counted) and only then with a rather weaker, but piercing sound does the Orthodox church announce the hour, and chime its own 2 a.m. A moment after it the tower clock on the Bey's mosque strikes the hour in a hoarse, faraway voice, and that strikes 11, the ghostly Turkish hour, by the strange calculation of distant and alien parts of the world."
4   Carlo Maria Martini, *Verso Gerusalemme* (Milan: Feltrinelli, 2002), 22–23.
5   Paul Virilio, *City of Panic*, trans. Julie Rose (Oxford: Berg, 2005), 11.
6   'Michel' is a pseudonym, used out of respect for his wish to remain unnamed, to preserve his anonymity.
7   Numbers vary from at least one hundred victims, as mentioned by Benny Morris, one of the champions of Israeli revisionist history, to the two hundred and fifty-four listed by the *New York Times* correspondent in Jerusalem, in an article published as soon as the news of the massacre spread.
8   Benny Morris, *The Birth of the Palestinian Refugee Problem Revisited* (Cambridge: Cambridge University Press, 2004), 255.
9   Meron Benvenisti, *Sacred Landscape: The Buried History of the Holy Land since 1948* (Berkeley: University of California Press, 2000), 116.

10 Avi Schlaim, *Lion of Jordan: The Life of King Hussein in War and Peace* (London: Penguin, 2007), 32.
11 Moshe Dayan, *Story of My Life* (London: Weidenfeld & Nicolson, 1976), 158.
12 Kai Bird, *Crossing Mandelbaum Gate: Coming of Age between the Arabs and Israelis, 1956–1978* (New York: Scribner, 2010), 23–24.
13 Roberto Alajmo, *Palermo*, trans. Guido Waldman (London: Haus, 2010).
14 Roberto Mazza, *Jerusalem: From the Ottomans to the British* (London: I.B. Tauris, 2009).
15 Victor Guérin, *La Terre Sainte: Jerusalem, et le nord de la Judee* (Paris: Librairie Plon, 1897), 6. Translation author's own.
16 Guerin, *La Terre Sainte*, 6.
17 Salim Tamari, *Mountain against the Sea: Essays on Palestinian Society and Culture* (Berkeley: University of California Press, 2009), 73. See also, Salim Tamari, ed., *Jerusalem 1948: The Arab Neighborhoods and Their Fate in the War* (Jerusalem: Institute of Jerusalem Studies and Badil Resource Center, 2002).
18 Haim Hanegbi and Tzachi Ostrovsky, "Palestinian Houses in West Jerusalem: Stories and Photographs," http://zochrot.org/uploads/uploads/27dc322c936-7a805c2bc69ef0ad1039d.pdf. The Amzalegs were British citizens, bankers, and, like the Moyal family, represented some Sephardic families living in Jerusalem under the Ottoman Empire, before the waves of Ashkenazi Zionist immigration.
19 Tamari, *Mountain against the Sea*, 182.
20 Joseph B. Glass and Ruth Kark, *Sephardi Entrepreneurs in Jerusalem: The Valero Family 1800–1948* (Jerusalem: Gefen, 2007), 169.
21 Amy Horowitz, *Mediterranean Israeli Music and the Politics of the Aesthetic* (Detroit, MI: Wayne State University Press, 2010), 38.
22 Roger Friedland and Richard Hecht, *To Rule Jerusalem* (Berkeley: University of California Press, 2000), 85.
23 Friedland and Hecht, *To Rule Jerusalem*, 85.
24 On the political demands and historical trajectory of the *panterim*, see, Deborah Bernstein, "The Black Panthers—Conflict and Protest in Israeli Society," *Youth and Society* 16 (1984): 129–52; Oz Frankel, "What's in a Name? The Black Panthers in Israel," *The Sixties: A Journal of History, Politics, and Culture* 1 (2008): 9–26.
25 Gideon N. Giladi, *Discord in Zion* (London: Scorpion, 1990).
26 Shlomo Hasson, *Urban Social Movements in Jerusalem: The Protest of the Second Generation* (Albany: State University of New York Press, 1993), 21.
27 Center for Jewish Community Studies, *Project Renewal: An Introduction to the Issues and Actors* (January 1980), 19.
28 Dick Gunther, *How High Is Up?* (Austin, TX: Emerald Book, 2009), 153.
29 Interview by the author with David Guggenheim, Jerusalem, December 7, 2010.
30 Roland Barthes, "Semiology and the Urban," in *Rethinking Architecture: A Reader in Cultural Theory*, ed. Neil Leach (London: Routledge, 1997), 168.
31 Michele Piccirillo, "Cosa ne è diventato di Betlemme?," December 23, 2005, http://www.appuntisugerusalemme.it/Dati/Che%20ne%20%C3%A8%20 diventato%20di%20Betlemme.htm. Author's translation.
   Fr. Michele Piccirillo (1944–2008) was a Franciscan priest who lived in the Old City of Jerusalem from 1964 until his death. A biblical scholar, field archaeologist, mosaic specialist, Greek epigraphist, and restoration expert of the Christian Holy Land, he led the small parish on Mount Nebo.
32 Meron Benvenisti, *City of Stone: The Hidden History of Jerusalem* (Berkeley: University of California Press, 1996), 136.
33 Benvenisti, *City of Stone: The Hidden History of Jerusalem*, 137.

34 By year's end 2014, Jerusalem's population of 870,000 was made up as follows: 534,000 Jews and others (63%), and 316,000 Arabs (37%). Israeli Central Bureau of Statistics, "Selected Data on the Occasion of Jerusalem Day (2014–2015)," http://www.cbs.gov.il/www/hodaot2016n/11_16_163e.pdf.

35 Alessandro Petti, "Asymmetries. The road network in Israel-Palestine," 10, http://www.decolonizing.ps/site/wp-content/uploads/2010/03/petti-a-asymmetries.pdf. Petti's article contains some of his thoughts articulated in his Italian volume: Alessandro Petti, *Arcipelaghi e enclave: Architetture dell'ordinamento spaziale contemporaneo* (Milan: Bruno Mondadori, 2007).

36 Helga Tawil-Souri, "Qalandia Checkpoint: The Historical Geography of a Non-Place," *Jerusalem Quarterly* 42 (2010): 26–48.

37 Augé, *Non-Places*, 64.

38 Hagar Kotef and Merav Amir, "(En)Gendering Checkpoints: Checkpoint Watch and the Repercussions of Intervention," *Signs: Journal of Culture and Society* 32 (2007): 982.

39 Augé, *Non-Places*, 83.

40 Zygmunt Bauman, "From Pilgrim to Tourist—or a Short History of Identity," in *Questions of Cultural Identity*, ed. Stuart Hall and Paul du Gay (London: Sage, 1996), 27. Cf. Mona Abaza, "Egyptianizing the American Dream: Nasr City's Shopping Mall, Public Order and the Privatized Military," in *Cairo Cosmopolitan: Politics, Culture and Urban Space in the New Globalized Middle East*, ed. Diane Singerman and Paul Amar (Cairo: The American University in Cairo Press, 2006); Tom Segev, *Elvis in Jerusalem: Post-Zionism and the Americanization of Israel* (New York: Metropolitan Books, 2001).

41 Walter Benjamin, *The Arcades Project*, trans. Howard Eiland and Kevin McLaughlin (Cambrige, Mass., and London, England: The Belknap Press of Harvard University Press, 2002), 10.

42 Author's interview with James Montague, February 6, 2012.

43 Quoted in Benny Morris, *The Birth of the Palestinian Refugee Problem Revisited* (Cambridge: Cambridge University Press, 2004), 393.

44 Benny Morris, *The Birth of the Palestinian Refugee Problem Revisited*, 393.

45 Italo Calvino, *Invisible Cities*, trans. William Weaver (New York: Harcourt Brace Jovanovich, 1974), 51.

46 Italo Calvino, *Invisible Cities*, trans. William Weaver (New York: Harcourt Brace Jovanovich, 1974), 51.

47 Calvino, *Invisible Cities*, 52.

48 Roland Barthes, "Semiology and the Urban," in *Rethinking Architecture: A Reader in Cultural Theory*, ed. Neil Leach (London: Routledge, 1997).

49 Deuteronomy (34:1–4), *The New Oxford Annotated Bible* (Oxford: Oxford University Press, 1973).

50 Translation author's own. See, http://www.sermig.org/it/nponline/166-np/1999-michele-piccirillo-una-vita-per-la-terra-santa.

51 B'Tselem, "The E1 Plan and Its Implications for Human Rights in the West Bank," December 2, 2012, http://www.btselem.org/settlements/20121202-_e1_human_rights_ramifications.

52 United Nations Special Committee on Palestine, "Recommendations to the UN General Assembly," UN Doc. A/364 (September 3, 1947), in *Documents on Jerusalem*, vol. IV, ed. Mahdi Abdul Hadi (Jerusalem: PASSIA, 2007), 5.

53 United Nations Special Committee on Palestine, "Recommendations to the UN General Assembly," UN Doc. A/364 (September 3, 1947), in *Documents on Jerusalem*, vol. IV, ed. Mahdi Abdul Hadi (Jerusalem: PASSIA, 2007), 5.

54 United Nations Special Committee on Palestine, "Recommendations to the UN General Assembly," UN Doc. A/364 (September 3, 1947), in *Documents on Jerusalem*, vol. IV, ed. Mahdi Abdul Hadi (Jerusalem: PASSIA, 2007), 5.

55 "UN General Assembly Resolution 181, 29 November 1947: Plan of Partition with Economic Union," in *Documents on Jerusalem*, vol. IV, ed. Mahdi Abdul Hadi (Jerusalem: PASSIA, 2007), 10.

56 Letter written by Br. George, February 6, 1963, in College des Freres archives, New Gate, Jerusalem. Author's translation.

57 Maoz Azaryahu, "Naming the Past: The Significance of Commemorative Street Names," in *Critical Toponymies: The Contested Politics of Place Naming*, ed. Lawrence D. Berg and Jani Vuolteenaho (Farnham: Ashgate, 2009), 54.

58 Azaryahu, "Naming the Past," 56.

59 Ira Sharkansky, *Governing Jerusalem: Again on the World's Agenda* (Detroit, MI: Wayne State University Press, 1996), 77.

60 Avishai Margalit, "The Myth of Jerusalem," in *Views in Review: Politics and Culture in the State of the Jews* (New York: Farrar, Straus and Giroux, 1998), 177–204.

61 Quoted in B'Tselem, *A Policy of Discrimination: Land Expropriation, Planning and Building in East Jerusalem* (May 1995), 34.

62 Quoted in B'Tselem, *A Policy of Discrimination*, 16.

63 United Nations Office for the Coordination of Humanitarian Affairs in the Palestinian Occupied Territory, *Sheikh Jarrah* (August 2009), 1.

64 Author's interview with Daniel Louria, September 10, 2004.

65 Meron Rapoport, *Shady Dealings in Silwan* (Jerusalem: Ir Amim, 2009), 7.

66 Rapoport, *Shady Dealings in Silwan*, 11.

67 Rapoport, *Shady Dealings in Silwan*, 28

68 Michael Dumper, *The Politics of Jerusalem since 1967* (New York: Columbia University Press, 1997), 11.

69 Nadia Abu el Haj, *Facts on the Ground: Archaeological Practice and Territorial Self-Fashioning in Israeli Society* (Chicago, IL: University of Chicago Press, 2001), 165.

70 Simone Ricca, *Reinventing Jerusalem: Israel's Reconstruction of the Jewish Quarter after 1967* (London: I.B. Tauris, 2007), 118.

71 European Union Heads of Mission, *European Union Heads of Mission Jerusalem Report 2012*, 1.

72 Salvo Licata, "La città azolo," unpublished text. Author's translation.

73 European Union Heads of Mission, *European Union Heads of Mission Jerusalem Report, 2012*, 1.

74 European Union Heads of Mission, *EU HOMS Report on Jerusalem* (2014), 2.

75 Stephen Bennett, "Jerusalem as Text: Taking Barthes to Town," *Jerusalem Quarterly* 52 (2011): 81.

76 Walter Benjamin, *The Work of Art in the Age of Its Technological Reproducibility, and Other Writings on Media*, eds. Michael W. Jennings, Brigid Doherty, and Thomas Y. Levin (Cambridge/London: The Belknap Press of Harvard University Press, 2008), 22.

77 David Horovitz, "Jerusalem Mayor Says the City's in the Fast Lane," *The Times of Israel*, February 11, 2013, http://www.timesofisrael.com/jerusalem-mayor-says-the-citys-in-the-fast-lane.

78 Avishai Margalit, "The Myth of Jerusalem," *New York Review of Books*, December 1991.

79 Laleh Khalili, "Virtual Nation: Palestinian Cyberculture in Lebanese Camps," in *Palestine, Israel, and the Politics of Popular Culture*, ed. Rebecca L. Stein and Ted Swedenburg (Durham, NC: Duke University Press, 2005), 126–49.

80 Sami Michael, *Victoria* (London: Macmillan, 1995).